# COST ACCOUNTING:
## A Canadian Management Guide

# COST ACCOUNTING:

## A CANADIAN MANAGEMENT GUIDE

JAMES W. VAIR, *B. Com., C.A.,*
*R.I.A., M.I.M.C.*

McGraw-Hill Company of Canada Limited
Toronto    *Montreal    New York    London*
*Sydney    Mexico    Johannesburg    Panama*
*Düsseldorf    Singapore    Rio de Janeiro*
*Kuala Lumpur    New Delhi*

COST ACCOUNTING:
A Canadian Management Guide

ISBN 0-07-092816-9
Library of Congress Catalog
Card Number 77-141827

1234567890 AP-71 0987654321

Printed and bound in Canada.

# ACKNOWLEDGMENTS

Although only six replies are reproduced in their entirety in Appendix B, the author wishes to record his sincere appreciation to all the individuals who took the time to compose a written answer to the questionnaire which provided the basis for the survey mentioned in Chapter 1, namely: W. Breckenridge, W. C. Brookes, M. H. Costa, G. H. Johnson, R. A. C. Knox, D. L. McClocklin, H. A. Moulds, W. S. Nurse, J. R. Pinchin, F. G. Stanley, R. C. Waddingham and W. L. B. Watts.

My special thanks to John W. Ross, B. Comm., M.B.A., R.I.A., Director of Research, the Society of Industrial Accountants of Canada, and to Philip W. B. Creighton, M.A. (Oxon.), F.C.A., Chairman of the Accounting Department, Centennial College of Applied Arts and Technology, Scarborough, for reading the draft manuscript and contributing many constructive suggestions. Any shortcomings that remain are entirely my own.

# PREFACE

The thesis of this modest book is that Cost Accounting is a collection of simple arithmetical techniques. That is, stripped of the vast superstructure of prose which clothes most of the standard texts on the subject, certain basic principles and practices can be isolated and described in a manner which facilitates their understanding by the student or business executive.

A perusal of a standard text on Cost Accounting can often be a frustrating experience for a business manager whose background may not be primarily financial. After reading several chapters, in all likelihood, he is still without the answer to the question that prompted his search in the first instance, while the jargon of the subject has probably given rise to a firm conviction that Cost Accounting is something better left to cost accountants. Thus an unhappy first brush with Cost Accounting can lead to a lasting under-appreciation of the usefulness of its techniques, many of which are appearing today under new names and new guises, and are being applied in areas far removed from the manufacturing operations where their value was first demonstrated — for example, Direct Costing, Responsibility Accounting, Distribution Costing and Functional Budgeting, to mention some of the important offshoots of conventional Cost Accounting.

What is required, then, if management is to gain a real appreciation of the contribution that Cost Accounting can make in steering the organization towards its planned objectives, is a better understanding of what Cost Accounting has to offer and how it is applied. At the same time, the value of costing techniques and the degree of rapport between top management and the cost department (or perhaps the individual cost accountant in a small enterprise) will be greatly enhanced if both parties have the same understanding of the purpose of the costs being produced. Hopefully this brief exploration will help to promote such understanding.

*James W. Vair*

# CONTENTS

# ONE

## WHAT IS COST?

Before attempting to answer this question, the writer conducted an informal survey among a select group of rather sophisticated business people comprising professional accountants as well as business executives who have had occasion to be involved with cost systems, or at least the output from a cost accounting system. In essence, the survey simply asked the individuals in the test sample to state their understanding of the terms *cost* and *cost accounting* without referring to an accounting dictionary or textbook in formulating the answer. Needless to say, the answers were remarkable for their diversity; yet, strangely enough, each one was almost entirely correct within the frame of reference that determined the application of cost statistics or a cost accounting system according to the respondent's understanding. In any event, the survey results emphasized a basic principle: *different costs are required for different purposes.* This concept is sometimes rather difficult for business managers to accept. They tend to feel, perhaps instinctively, that there must be *one true cost* for any given product or any specific item of tangible or intangible property or service, and that cost accountants are remarkably inefficient as a group if they cannot arrive at this idealistic figure. This misunderstanding, when it arises, is simply the result of an information gap between the cost accountant and the layman, a gap which, hopefully, should not be too difficult to bridge.

If we trace the beginnings of Cost Accounting, we find that it originated in the factory, the plant or the works, as it is variously referred to (the latter term being most commonly employed in the United Kingdom where there is a professional body called The Institute of Cost and Works Accountants Ltd.). Why was this so? Most probably because of the limitations of conventional accounting methods for arriving at the "Cost of Goods Manufactured" figure in a manufacturing or production environ-

1

ment. To illustrate, consider the typical statement of a business which manufactures some or all of the goods which it sells:

## Figure 1.

### THE OLD-LINE MANUFACTURING COMPANY

### STATEMENT OF COST OF GOODS MANUFACTURED
Year ended December 31, 19—

| | | |
|---|---:|---:|
| Inventory of work-in-process, January 1, 19— | | $ 100,000 |
| Cost of Materials used: | | |
|   Inventory of raw materials, January 1, 19— | $120,000 | |
|   Purchases | 810,000 | |
|   Freight-in | 25,000 | |
| | $955,000 | |
|   Inventory of raw materials, December 31, 19— | 105,000 | 850,000 |
| Direct Labour | | 735,000 |
| Factory Overhead Expenses: | | |
|   Supervision | $ 50,000 | |
|   Indirect labour | 180,500 | |
|   Factory supplies | 10,600 | |
|   Light, heat, power & water | 46,400 | |
|   Miscellaneous factory expense items | 28,000 | 315,500 |
| | | $2,000,500 |
| Inventory of work-in-process, December 31, 19— | | 93,500 |
| *Cost of Goods Manufactured* | | $1,907,000 |

After arriving at a value for Cost of Goods Manufactured, the next step is to transfer these "factory costs" into the Operating Statement, the Income Statement, or the Statement of Profit & Loss as it is variously termed, in order to ascertain if the business has realized a net gain or loss on the operations for the year. (See Figure 2. opposite.)

One of the more confusing features of these statements (at least to the uninitiated) is that we are always adding and deducting some sort of inventory. Thus, before arriving at the "Gross Trading Margin" line, three inventories at the beginning of the year have been added to costs and three inventories at the end of the year have been deducted. Can you find them all? The fact is, in the absence of a cost accounting system there is simply no way of determining the operating results for a manufacturing business without taking stock and arriving at a valuation for all these inventories. Can you visualize doing this every month-end in order to produce a monthly profit and loss statement? In most companies the expense of this sort

**Figure 2.**

THE OLD-LINE MANUFACTURING COMPANY
STATEMENT OF PROFIT & LOSS
Year ended December 31, 19—

| | | |
|---|---|---:|
| Net Sales | | $3,240,000 |
| Cost of Goods Sold: | | |
| Inventory of finished goods, January 1, 19— | $ 108,000 | |
| Cost of Goods Manufactured (Per Statement) | 1,907,000 | |
| | $2,015,000 | |
| Inventory of finished goods, December 31, 19— | 116,500 | 1,898,500 |
| Gross Trading Margin | | $1,341,500 |
| Selling & Administrative Expenses: | | |
| Selling expenses | $ 644,600 | |
| Administrative expenses | 360,900 | 1,005,500 |
| Profit before taxes thereon | | $ 336,000 |
| Provision for income taxes | | 169,500 |
| *Net profit for year* | | $ 166,500 |

of cost-finding would be prohibitive and, as a result, it is simply not done. Instead, estimates are made of the gross margin realized on sales based on prior experience, and a physical count of raw materials, work-in-process and finished goods on hand is made once or twice a year. This is why so many small and not-so-small businesses in North America are literally "flying blind" with the aid of only the most crude navigational aids.

Another limitation of the statements cited in our example is that they deal entirely with large aggregations of revenue and cost. This shortcoming may not be apparent unless your curiosity has been aroused as to what kind of business is being conducted by THE OLD-LINE MANUFACTURING COMPANY. However, if you have just recently become a shareholder, you would probably like to know if the sales figure represents 3,240,000 screw drivers sold for a dollar each or 30 power shovels priced at $108,000 per machine. In addition, you would obviously like to know if this is a one-product business or if a variety of products and services are being produced and sold. The latter is most probably the case, since even in this age of specialization, it is a rarity indeed to find a business that has all its eggs in one basket.

The preceding general accounting statements in conventional form serve to illustrate two rather significant attributes of *cost*. Firstly, there is a wide variety of costs associated with an industrial enterprise (or with any kind of business, for that matter), and it is important to define precisely what costs are under study in any particular case. Selling and Administration

Expenses, for example, fall just as logically into the category of *costs* as Factory Overhead Expenses, although the former have been considered traditionally "off limits" to the cost accountant until recent years. Secondly, there is an obvious need to develop unit costs under many circumstances — to facilitate the pricing of inventories, to assess the profitability of a given product, or to establish market prices for new or changed products, to cite some of the most obvious reasons.

At this point, the reader probably understands at least that *costs* are the opposite of *revenue* (as represented by *sales,* for example). In other words, *costs* represent outlays or expenditures, and this is the way the term *cost* is defined by The Canadian Institute of Chartered Accountants in a useful little book called *Accounting Terminology.*

> *cost.* The outlay made or the obligation incurred, as measured
> in terms of money, to obtain property or services.[1]

It is, of course, possible to quibble over this definition (either it is too condensed or too all-embracing) as with any of the several dozen others to be found in current authoritative works on the subject of Cost Accounting. However, such "nit-picking" would serve no useful purpose in promoting an understanding of the nature of costs. The definition quoted has the virtue of brevity and serves to make clear the basic point that a cost represents an outlay of some form or other. Rather than debate the merits of each of the commonly used terms in Cost Accounting and General Accounting, a more constructive approach is to make an analytical survey of the costs which are developed in any given organization.

At this point, it is useful to state a fundamental theorem:

> All the costs of an organization represent a structure com-
> posed of several or many levels, the highest level being *the
> total costs of the period,* and the lowest level representing
> *elementary costs* which are not further subdivided within
> the accounting system maintained by the organization.

Taking this approach, all the costs that are developed within a company fall into a logical interrelationship with one another.

Earlier it was stated that there is a wide variety of costs associated with a business, irrespective of the nature of the enterprise. This statement is correct insofar as it goes, but it may be more precise to state, in the light of the above theorem, that there are many levels of cost within an organization. At the same time, redefinition of costs is also possible at any level.

This last statement simply means that there are more ways than one to analyze a given level or group of costs, as a little reflection will show. Thus, a corporate manager might like to know what his costs are by territory or by salesman, as well as by product.

Mention was also made of unit costs in discussing the attributes of cost.

Referring again to the above theorem, you might guess that unit costs represent *elementary costs*. Generally speaking, this is true in a great many businesses, although it should be recognized that the term *unit cost* is also subject to qualification. Thus, the unit cost of a product, for example, may be further analyzed into the cost of its component parts or subassemblies, in which case the unit cost would then be a *group cost* and the components would be the *elementary costs*. However, this complexity is one that can be ignored for the moment.

**Figure 3.**

| LEVEL: | 01 | 02 | |
|---|---|---|---|
| | TOTAL COSTS OF THE PERIOD $3,073,500 | INCOME TAXES | $169,500 |
| | | ADMIN. EXPENSES | $360,900 |
| | | SELLING EXPENSES | $644,600 |
| | | COST OF GOODS SOLD | $1,898,500 |

Returning to our model enterprise, THE OLD-LINE MANUFACTUR-ING COMPANY, the financial statements of this business implicitly declare three levels of costs. The first two levels are contained wholly within the Statement of Profit & Loss, Figure 2, and may conveniently be displayed in the form of a structure, as set forth in Figure 3. For convenience in notation, the highest level is assigned a level number of 01 and lower levels are designated as 02, 03 and so on.

For the benefit of any readers who may be experienced accountants, and therefore likely to be concerned with the balancing features of the cost structure illustrated, we may summarize the figures in tabular form with the addition of percentages to give a better picture of the relative magnitude of the several components involved:

|  | AMOUNT | % |
|---|---|---|
| Cost of Goods Sold | $1,898,500 | 61.8 |
| Selling expenses | 644,600 | 21.0 |
| Administrative expenses | 360,900 | 11.7 |
| Income taxes | 169,500 | 5.5 |
| Total Costs of the Period | $3,073,500 | 100.0 |

. . . and if anyone doubts that $3,073,500 is, in fact, all the costs incurred by THE OLD-LINE MANUFACTURING COMPANY, we may insert this figure in a simple relation test with the Net Sales for the period to arrive at the Net Profit previously developed:

| Net Sales | $3,240,000 |
|---|---|
| Total Costs (as above) | 3,073,500 |
| Net Profit for year | $ 166,500 |

The third level of costs declared by the financial statements of our sample company is contained in the Statement of Cost of Goods Manufactured (Figure 1) and represents a number of cost items subsidiary to the group cost figure "Cost of Goods Sold," which is itself a cost structure. This is illustrated in Figure 4. opposite.

Again, the components of the Level 03 costs may be summarized in tabular form, as follows:

|  | AMOUNT | % |
|---|---|---|
| Net decrease in inventories | $ 13,000 | 0.7 |
| Materials purchased, including freight-in | 835,000 | 44.0 |
| Direct labour | 735,000 | 38.7 |
| Factory overhead expenses | 315,500 | 16.6 |
| Cost of Goods Sold | $1,898,500 | 100.0 |

The item "net decrease in inventories" is simply a convenient way of summarizing the effect on Cost of Goods Sold of variations between the inventories of raw materials, work-in-process and finished goods at the

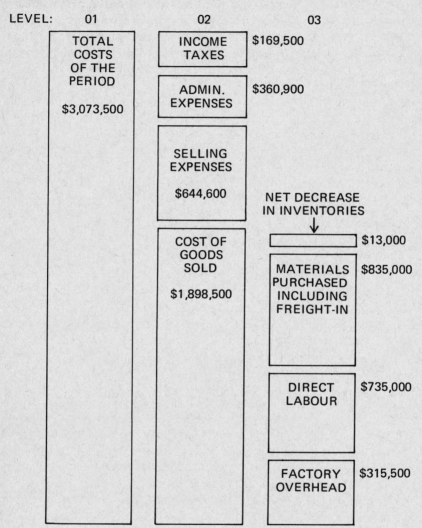

Figure 4.

LEVEL: 01         02         03

TOTAL COSTS OF THE PERIOD

$3,073,500

INCOME TAXES — $169,500

ADMIN. EXPENSES — $360,900

SELLING EXPENSES — $644,600

NET DECREASE IN INVENTORIES — $13,000

COST OF GOODS SOLD — $1,898,500

MATERIALS PURCHASED INCLUDING FREIGHT-IN — $835,000

DIRECT LABOUR — $735,000

FACTORY OVERHEAD — $315,500

beginning and end of the accounting period — in this case, one year. It is calculated in this manner:

| | RAW MATERIALS | WORK-IN-PROCESS | FINISHED GOODS | TOTAL |
|---|---|---|---|---|
| Inventory, January 1 | $120,000 | $100,000 | $108,000 | $328,000 |
| Inventory, December 31 | 105,000 | 93,500 | 116,500 | 315,000 |
| Net (increase)/decrease | $ 15,000 | $ 6,500 | $ (8,500) | $ 13,000 |

The above little algorithm is not an argument against the *step form* in which inventories are dealt with in conventional or general accounting statements; it is simply a more convenient method in this case for deriving the net change that has occurred in the inventory balances between the beginning and end of the year. It is also a reminder of the steps that have to be performed in the absence of a cost accounting system in order to arrive at the operating results for a given period, as was mentioned earlier.

Another way of thinking about the flow of costs through an organization that helps to promote an understanding of the process is to visualize each of the inventory accounts — raw materials, work-in-process and finished goods — as a series of buckets. At the beginning of the accounting period, each of these buckets holds a certain quantity of product having a determinable value: the opening inventory. Throughout the year, additional quantities of materials and/or services are being continually added, while each bucket in the series is also continually dumping its contents into the next bucket along the line, the final bucket usually being given the label, "Cost of Goods Sold." Reduced to its simplest terms, this is the way a cost accounting system operates. That is, it records the inputs and outputs from each bucket and also keeps track of the levels remaining at regular intervals.

By contrast, in a general accounting system there is usually no continuous measurement of inputs except to the extent that they involve purchases from outsiders or outlays involving disbursement of cash, such as payments for wages or certain overhead expenses. As a result, it is possible to determine the aggregate inputs that have gone into the system as a whole, but since internal transfers are ignored or only partially recorded, it is necessary to measure the level in each bucket from time to time in order to develop meaningful figures for the outputs. This is the tedious and time-consuming feature mentioned earlier that makes a cost accounting system a rather attractive alternative to a general accounting system, at least in a manufacturing environment.

The question may have occurred to some astute reader at this point — is there a relationship between a cost structure as described earlier and the concept of a series of buckets through which the costs of the enterprise flow? They are certainly interdependant, and both an inventory account and a cost structure display certain values at a given point of time. In other words, they provide what has been aptly described as a photograph of the business at a certain date. It is not expected that these values will remain constant from day to day, or even that they will keep the same proportions to each other from one accounting period to another. For example, the "net (increase)/decrease in inventories" figure could easily have been a negative or credit balance — as indeed it was in the case of one of the elements comprising the net figure of $13,000 developed in the example above, namely, the net change in the Finished Goods inventory. As will be seen later, it is quite possible for certain costs to have negative or credit balances from time to time, and the concept of a cost structure is not changed because certain of the elements comprising it have different signs — plus or minus, or *debit* or *credit,* as they are termed in the language of accounting.

Finally, it is necessary to recognize that the series of buckets, as they are somewhat inelegantly termed above, are really temporary containers or holding accounts set up for convenience in classifying and controlling the flow of costs through the organization. Each one of these buckets with the exception of the last one (Cost of Goods Sold) is an inventory account, and hence an asset of the business until the products or services which they hold have been sold to third parties. At this point they lose their ambivalence and become true cost elements to be matched against the revenue or income derived from their sale. While it is not the purpose of this modest work to cover the whole field of accounting theory, the following definition from the book, *Accounting Terminology* may help to clarify the point:

> *inventory.* In accounting terminology, the word is usually restricted to designate items of tangible personal property which are held for sale in the ordinary course of business, or are in the process of production for such sale, or are to be currently consumed in the production of goods or services to be available for sale.[2]

If there is any conclusion to be drawn from the foregoing it is that the term *cost* has a variety of meanings depending upon the circumstances under which it is used, and it is important to recognize that different costs are required for different purposes. Further, when looking at the operations of any particular organization, the concept of a *cost structure* is a useful analytical tool in sorting out the interrelationships that exist between different levels of cost and different types of cost within the business under study.

Two of the most serious limitations of General Accounting, (1) the failure to analyze costs in sufficient detail to permit a satisfactory degree of management control, and (2) the necessity for taking a complete physical inventory in order to develop an accurate statement of operating results, can, it is suggested, be overcome through the technique of cost accounting. That is, Cost Accounting provides a means of measuring and controlling the flow of costs through an enterprise besides giving useful status information with respect to inventories at appropriate dates, such as the end of a month or other interim accounting period.

● REFERENCES

1. *Accounting Terminology,* The Canadian Institute of Chartered

Accountants, Toronto, 1957, p.20.

2.  *Ibid,* p.38.

- QUESTIONS AND CASE PROBLEMS

In the case of the first and subsequent chapters, a distinction is not made between a question and a case problem. The dichotomy would be simply a matter of subjective judgment and of doubtful value to the reader. As a rough guide to selection, however, it may be stated that the exercises are in approximate order of difficulty.

1.01  Without referring to Appendix B, give brief definitions, using your own words, for the terms *cost* and *cost accounting.*

1.02  Compare your answers for 1.01 with the six replies in Appendix B. Do you agree or disagree with any of the statements made? (Give reasons in each case.)

1.03  Name the principal features of a Cost Accounting System that distinguish it from a General Accounting System.

1.04  What are *factory costs?*

1.05  Why is it desirable to develop *unit costs* and what value do they have?

1.06  Assuming that the sales of the OLD-LINE MANUFACTURING COMPANY do, in fact, represent 30 power shovels priced at $108,000 each, what is the average cost per machine, to the nearest dollar?

1.07  The spread between the selling price and the cost of a product is usually termed the "gross margin" with reference to the selling price, and the "mark-up" with reference to the cost. Using the data from 1.06 above, express as a percentage:

(a)  the gross margin on sales;

(b)  the mark-up on cost.

1.08  You are asked to prepare a condensed Statement of Profit & Loss for last year but you are not supplied with a schedule of Cost of Goods Sold. Can you prepare such a statement from the following data? (Illustrate)

|  | DR | CR |
| --- | --- | --- |
| Gross trading margin | | $1,341,500 |
| Selling expenses | $644,600 | |
| Administrative expenses | 360,900 | |
| Provision for income taxes | 169,500 | |

1.09 If a manufacturing company charges all the wages and salaries of its factory personnel to Direct Labour, what effect does this have on its cost structure, and ultimately the financial reports of the business?

1.10 What is the function of an inventory account, and why is the analogy of a bucket appropriate to describe such an account?

1.11 If all the products manufactured by an enterprise are sold as soon as they are produced, is there any need for inventory accounts?

1.12 In a manufacturing business, name the inventories that generally must be counted, priced and extended, in the absence of a cost accounting system, in order that financial statements may be prepared showing the operating results for the period.

1.13 If the profit for the year in a manufacturing business amounts to $240,000 before the inventories at the beginning and end of the year are taken into account, what will the final profit figure be if there has been a "net decrease in inventories" of $15,000? (Explain).

1.14 What are some of the important internal transfers that are not accounted for in a General Accounting System?

1.15 The COST OF GOODS SOLD in a local branch plant is made up of PAPER CUPS, TRADING GOODS and OTHER COST OF SALES. Some of these items are broken down further: PAPER CUPS is made up of HOT DRINK CUPS, COLD DRINK CUPS and SUN-DAE CUPS; TRADING GOODS is made up of HOT FOOD DISHES and ICE CREAM DISHES.
Diagram the cost structures involved in this plant.

1.16 The SELLING EXPENSES of $644,600 declared in Figure 3 are divisible into 4 districts, as follows:

DISTRICT #1 — 30%
#2 — 35%
#3 — 10%
#4 — 25%

Each district is in turn divided into territories by salesmen. For example, District #4 is serviced by 3 salesmen whose expense budgets are:

SALESMAN A — $52,150
B — 65,000
C — 44,000

Draw a cost structure along the lines of Figure 4 giving a level number of 02 to SELLING EXPENSES, a level number of 03 to DISTRICT COSTS, and a level number of 04 to TERRITORY

COSTS. It is not necessary to make the boxes precisely proportionate in size; just concentrate on getting the correct dollar values assigned to each cost element involved.

1.17  Specify some of the ways in which the sales and cost of goods sold may be analyzed in a business in order to assist the management decision-making process.

# TWO

## HOW A COST ACCOUNTING
## SYSTEM* OPERATES

In the case of most integrated cost systems (integrated in the sense that the accounts used for cost accounting purposes are tied in with or controlled by the general accounting system), the underlying structural framework is quite similar and can usually be clearly discerned upon analysis. Such differences as do exist are mainly attributable to the manner in which unit costs are developed, a subject that will be probed in some depth when the different types of cost systems are examined.

A fairly simple model of a cost system is described by the schematic diagram in Figure 5. Inventory accounts (or "buckets" as they were referred to in the preceding Chapter) are identified by the flowerpot or bucket-shaped symbol, and costs structures are designated by rectangles. A somewhat more sophisticated model is illustrated in Figure 6. The latter indicates that the identity of the major elements of cost: raw materials, direct labour and factory overhead, is preserved in the process from the point of origin or entry to the final resting place in cost of goods sold. This breakdown by major cost elements is desirable for several reasons. As may be evident from their titles, the nature of each element is quite different, and hence, the accounting and control techniques that are appropriate for each element are necessarily different also. Another reason for preserving the distinction through each step of the process is that it facilitates the location of errors and balancing in the accounting sense. That is, the detailed subsidiary records by job, project, or department, for example, can more readily be agreed to or reconciled with the control totals represented by the balances in the inventory accounts or "buckets" when the materials, labour, overhead analysis is maintained throughout the system. Finally, in order to establish a satisfactory level of internal control within the organization or to create

---

*Hereafter referred to as a "cost system" for the sake of brevity.

**Figure 5.**

THE FLOW OF AGGREGATE COSTS IN A BUSINESS:
A Simple Model.

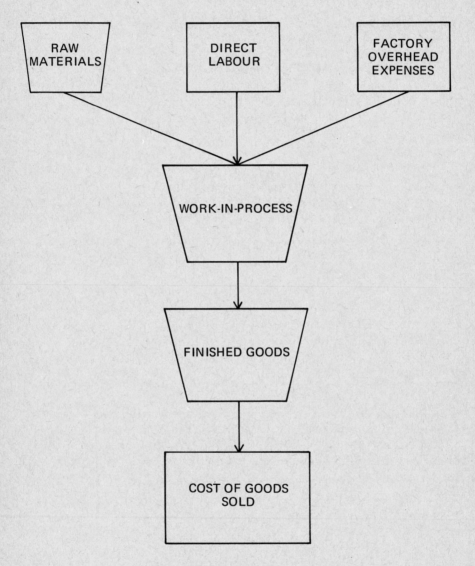

good audit-trails, it is rather important to be able to "prove" the figures developed by the cost system — by tracing the aggregate inputs for a given accounting period through the system to their final resting place in Cost of Goods Sold or in one or more of the inventory accounts.

To illustrate, let us assume that THE OLD-LINE MANUFACTURING

**Figure 6.**

THE FLOW OF AGGREGATE COSTS IN A BUSINESS:
A More Complex Model.

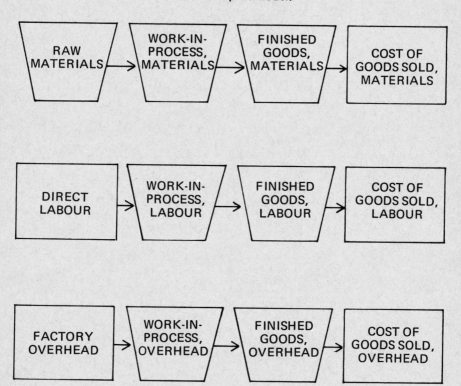

COMPANY does, in fact, have an integrated cost system (notwithstanding the format of the financial statements previously displayed).

Starting with the first "bucket," the raw materials inventory, we know that the opening balance at January 1, 19— was _____ $120,000

We are also told that purchases and freight-in amounted to $835,000 (we will defer discussion for the present as to whether or not it is appropriate to include freight-in as part of the laid-down cost of material purchases). Under an integrated cost system, such acquisitions of raw material would not be charged to an account termed "purchases" but directly to the raw materials inventory account. Adding the purchases for the year to the opening balance ($835,000 + $120,000) gives a total of _____ $955,000

At the same time, issues from stock amounting to $850,000 were made throughout the year ------------------------

$955,000
(850,000)

Under a cost system, greater precision in terminology is desirable, so we will describe these issues as "transfers to work-in-process." After giving effect to these "transfers," the new balance in raw materials inventory ($955,000 —$850,000) is -----------------------------------

$105,000

. . . which, happily, agrees with the figures shown in the Statement of Cost of Goods Manufactured (Figure 1.).

The point to be recognized is that the balance at December 31, 19— would be determined automatically by the cost system and a complete physical stocktaking would not be required to arrive at a value for the closing inventory *as well as* the issues or transfers to production for the year. Periodic checks of inventory balances developed by the cost system are, of course, desirable, but this is something that is usually done on a rotating basis covering portions of the inventory only on a given count date.

Passing on to the next step, the analysis of the flow of costs through work-in-process is as follows:

| | MATERIALS | LABOUR | OVERHEAD | TOTAL |
|---|---|---|---|---|
| Inventory, January 1, 19— | $ 45,000 | $ 39,000 | $ 16,000 | $ 100,000 |
| Material transfers (above) | 850,000 | — | — | 850,000 |
| Direct labour applied | — | 735,000 | — | 735,000 |
| Overhead applied | — | — | 315,500 | 315,500 |
| | $895,000 | $774,000 | $331,500 | $2,000,500 |
| Transferred to Finished Goods | 853,000 | 737,500 | 316,500 | 1,907,000 |
| Inventory, December 31, 19— | $ 42,000 | $ 36,500 | $ 15,000 | $ 93,500 |

Apparently our cost system is operating in a reasonably satisfactory manner, for most of the figures in the above tabulation are capable of reconciliation with the old-fashioned Statement of Cost of Goods Manufactured (Figure 1). The only detail you have to accept on faith is the analysis of the opening and closing inventories as between materials, labour and overhead. This analysis is always made by manufacturing companies (at least in their year-end inventories) even when they do not have an integrated cost system. However, there is no necessity for showing this detail in the conventional Statement of Cost of Goods Manufactured, so it is simply omitted in most cases.

Another feature that may have caught your eye is the use of the term "applied" in connection with the labour and overhead transfers in. The use of this term is deliberate to indicate that the amount of labour and overhead dumped into work-in-process is *not necessarily* the same as the actual amount incurred for each of these cost elements during the period under review. However, for the sake of simplicity in our illustration, we have assumed that the transfers to work-in-process for labour and overhead *are* the actual amounts incurred for the year, in the case of THE OLD-LINE MANUFACTURING COMPANY.

Finally, we come to the stage representing the whole purpose of the manufacturing operations carried on by the Company: the production of finished goods for sale. The movement in the finished goods inventory, then, may be analyzed in a similar fashion:

|  | MATERIALS | LABOUR | OVERHEAD | TOTAL |
|---|---|---|---|---|
| Inventory, January 1, 19— | $ 49,000 | $ 42,000 | $ 17,000 | $ 108,000 |
| Transferred from work-in-process (above) | 853,000 | 737,500 | 316,500 | 1,907,000 |
|  | $902,000 | $779,500 | $333,500 | $2,015,000 |
| Transferred to Cost of Goods Sold | 849,500 | 734,000 | 315,000 | 1,898,500 |
| Inventory, December 31, 19— | $ 52,500 | $ 45,500 | $ 18,500 | $ 116,500 |

Again, this schedule is capable of reconciliation, at least as regards the TOTAL column, with the Statement of Profit & Loss (Figure 2.). At this point, however, the resemblance ends, for it is definitely *not* the practice in companies that do not have an integrated cost system to identify the major cost elements that make up the total valuation of each individual item in their finished goods inventory. In fact, more often than not, a rather questionable practice is followed: the finished goods inventory value is arrived at by deducting the normal gross margin on the items in question from the selling price. Since the selling price is subject to variation because of a large number of factors that have nothing to do with the cost of production, this has the effect of burying random market fluctuations in the Cost of Goods Sold figure. This is not to dispute the necessity for an *inventory valuation account* under certain circumstances (to provide for those cases where the expected selling price less normal gross margin produces a valuation below cost of production), but such a provision should appear as a separate item in the operating statement, and not as an inflation of the current period's production costs. However, no such problem afflicts THE OLD-LINE MANUFACTURING COMPANY, so we may now restate the cost structure for Cost of Goods Sold (originally declared as a group of level 03 costs in Figure 4) as illustrated in Figure 7.

A comparison of this revised cost structure with the original indicates that the more refined costing has had the effect of allocating virtually all the "net decrease in inventories" to direct materials, the effect on direct labour (—$1,000) and overhead (—$500) being too small to change their respective proportions to the aggregate of Cost of Goods Sold by even 1/10 of 1%.

**Figure 7.**

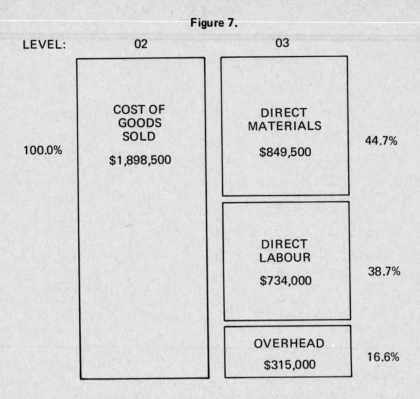

LEVEL:            02                    03

100.0%    COST OF GOODS SOLD $1,898,500    DIRECT MATERIALS $849,500    44.7%

DIRECT LABOUR $734,000    38.7%

OVERHEAD $315,000    16.6%

The maintenance of an integrated cost system, as you may have surmised by this point, can also have a significant effect on the regular financial statements of the business. Thus, since cost of sales figures are obtained automatically, there is really no need to prepare the conventional Statement of Cost of Goods Manufactured — unless one wishes to go through the reconciliation process mentioned earlier in connection with internal control and audit-trails. At the same time, the Profit & Loss Statement can be considerably "streamlined" through elimination of the tedious adding and subtracting of finished goods inventories:

## Figure 8.

### THE OLD-LINE MANUFACTURING COMPANY
### STATEMENT OF PROFIT & LOSS
Year ended December 31, 19—

| | | |
|---|---:|---:|
| Net Sales | | $3,240,000 |
| Cost of Goods Sold | | 1,898,500 |
| Gross Trading Margin | | $1,341,500 |
| Selling & Administrative Expenses: | | |
|    Selling expenses | $644,600 | |
|    Administrative expenses | 360,900 | 1,005,500 |
| Profit before taxes thereon | | $ 336,000 |
| Provision for income taxes | | 169,500 |
| *Net profit for year* | | $ 166,500 |

• QUESTIONS AND CASE PROBLEMS

2.01 The cost system of INTERGALACTIC LIMITED is an orthodox one with the added refinement that the Factory Overhead Expenses cost structure is divided into two parts: Variable Overhead and Fixed Overhead. The former is transferred to Work-In-Process along with the other major cost elements while the latter (Fixed Overhead) is simply added to Cost of Goods Sold and does not influence the valuation of the Finished Goods Inventory.

Draw a schematic diagram along the lines of Figure 5 showing how the cost system operates.

2.02 What are the advantages of preserving the identity of the major elements of cost through the input, processing and output phases of a cost system?

2.03 Subsequent to the preparation of the financial statements for the year ended December 31, 19—, THE OLD-LINE MANUFACTURING COMPANY discovered that part of the finished goods inventory is obsolete and will not realize the normal gross margin of 41.4%. In short, a reduction in the value of a portion of the finished goods inventory in the amount of $30,000 is required.

Re-draft the Statement of Profit & Loss as shown in Figure 8 to give effect to this adjustment. (Hint: the item should be shown as a "non-recurring charge" after all other expenses and before the Provision for Income Taxes which may now be reduced by 52% of the dollar amount of the adjustment.)

2.04  It is ascertained that the material issues of THE OLD-LINE MANU-FACTURING COMPANY during the year just ended have been costed using old prices which do not reflect an average increase of 7½% charged by suppliers throughout the year. Accordingly, it is proposed to adjust work-in-process, finished goods and cost of goods sold to correct this undercosting of material issues.

(a)  Calculate the amount of the adjustment required to each of the inventory accounts affected as well as to cost of goods sold.

(b)  Compute: (i) the net change in the "profit before taxes" which will result from this adjustment, (ii) the change required in the "provision for income taxes" assuming a tax rate of 52%, and (iii) the net effect on "net profit for the year."

2.05  A physical count of finished goods has revealed a shortage of $12,000 as compared to the book value of stock indicated to be on hand in the warehouse. This represents approximately 10% of the average balance on hand at any given month-end.

What action should be taken with respect to this shortage? (Discuss)

2.06  The SHORTCUT MACHINE SHOP does not bother to account for labour and overhead by individual jobs. Instead direct labour and shop overhead are applied on a standard formula basis as a fixed percentage of the material costs on each job, the percentages used being 85% for direct labour and 35% for shop overhead.
For the month of March, 19—, actual costs incurred were:

MATERIAL:

| Job — 302 | $ | 525 |
|---|---|---|
| — 303 | | 852 |
| — 305 | | 408 |
| — 306 | | 249 |
| — 307 | | 766 |
| — 310 | | 610 |
| — 311 | | 511 |
| — 312 | | 521 |
| — 313 | | 531 |
| — 314 | | 572 |
| | | $5,545 |

DIRECT LABOUR:

176 hours per man for a 10-man work force paid at an average rate of $2.60 per hour.

SHOP OVERHEAD:

| | |
|---|---|
| Supervision | $500 |
| Supplies | 418 |
| Fuel & utilities | 367 |
| Machinery repairs | 375 |

(a) Calculate the direct labour and shop overhead applied on the formulae bases and also the amounts under- or overapplied as compared with the actual costs incurred for the month.

(b) What do you think of SHORTCUT'S approach to labour and overhead costing by job? Is it sufficiently accurate?

2.07 The SHORTCUT MACHINE SHOP problem (2.06 above) illustrates the point that "the amount of labour and overhead applied is not necessarily the same as the actual amount incurred for each of these cost elements during the period under review."

How should SHORTCUT treat the amounts under- or overapplied in its accounts and financial statements?

2.08 POPULAR LADIESWEAR INC. has operated without formal cost accounting procedures for many years. In the current fiscal year commencing July 1, an integrated cost system was introduced, and the operating results for the first month on the new basis, which involves the determination of individual costs for each style and size of garment produced, were as follows:

### POPULAR LADIESWEAR INC.

### STATEMENT OF COST OF GOODS SOLD

Month of July, 19—

| | | | |
|---|---|---|---|
| Materials used | | | $17,700 |
| Direct labour | | | 7,000 |
| Overhead expenses | | | 6,800 |
| | | | $31,500 |
| Inventory, July 1: | | | |
| Work-in-process | | $13,200 | |
| Finished goods | | 13,500 | 26,700 |
| | | | $58,200 |
| Inventory, July 31: | | | |
| Work-in-process | | $ 7,900 | |
| Finished goods | | 8,000 | 15,900 |
| *Cost of goods sold* | | | $42,300 |

## INCOME STATEMENT
### Month of July, 19—

| | |
|---|---:|
| Sales | $60,000 |
| Cost of goods sold (per schedule) | 42,300 |
| Gross margin | $17,700 |
| Operating expenses | 11,900 |
| *Pre-Tax Profit* | $ 5,800 |

The President feels that the reported profit is low compared to the experience of prior years and wishes to "verify" the operating results by preparing an Income Statement on the old basis whereby finished goods and work-in-process were valued at selling price less normal gross profit. That is, finished goods were customarily estimated to cost 30% off selling price, while in the case of work-in-process, a further assumption was made that the garments in question were, on an average, 50% complete.

| Inventories at selling price were: | July 1 | July 31 |
|---|---|---|
| Work-in-process | $36,000 | $24,000 |
| Finished goods | 21,000 | 14,000 |

(a) Prepare a Statement of Cost of Goods Sold and an Income Statement on the "old basis."

(b) Which statements, in your opinion, reflect most accurately the results of operations for the month? (Give reasons)

2.09 The President of BULKY BOXES LIMITED, upon reviewing his financial statements for the year ended December 31, 19—, exclaimed: "Labour costs are siphoning off all our profits! If we didn't have such a low overhead, we wouldn't be able to stay in business."

A comparison of the condensed Income Statement of BULKY BOXES LIMITED with the published statistical averages for the industry is what prompted the President's remarks — namely:

| | BULKY BOXES LIMITED Year ended Dec. 31, | | INDUSTRY AVERAGES |
|---|---|---|---|
| | Dollars | (% of Sales) | (% of Sales) |
| Sales | $720,000 | 100.00 | 100.00 |
| Cost of Sales: | | | |
| Materials | $349,200 | 48.50 | 47.00 |
| Direct labour | 181,800 | 25.25 | 18.00 |
| Factory overhead | 77,400 | 10.75 | 15.00 |
| | $608,400 | 84.50 | 80.00 |
| Gross Margin | $111,600 | 15.50 | 20.00 |

However, there is some doubt concerning the accuracy of the above financial statement. For example, the following questionable distributions of expenses appear to have been made during the year:

— Machine repair parts totalling $14,400 were charged to Direct Material.

— The salary of the Factory Manager ($12,000) was charged to Direct Labour.

— Indirect labour involved in painting the factory and other maintenance jobs amounting to $13,300 were charged to Direct Labour.

— Vacation pay, unemployment insurance, Workmen's Compensation Board levies, and the Company's share of hospital and group life insurance aggregating $26,900 were all charged to Direct Labour.

(a) Prepare a revised Income Summary for the year after correcting the above errors in the distribution of certain expenses.

(b) What major cost element is apparently out of line with the Industry Averages based on the revised Income Summary prepared in (a) above? Is this a useful comparison?

2.10   The following is a schedule of the completed production of TRANS-POSITION INCORPORATED for the month of September, 19—

|  | RAW MATERIAL | DIRECT LABOUR | FACTORY OVERHEAD | TOTAL |
|---|---|---|---|---|
| Work-in-process, September 1 | $ 11,250 | $ 9,750 | $ 4,550 | |
| Materials issued | 232,575 | — | — | |
| Direct labour (actual) | — | 185,084 | — | |
| Factory overhead (actual) | — | — | 102,379 | |
| | $243,825 | $194,834 | $106,929 | |
| Transferred to finished goods | 212,911 | 183,834 | 79,005 | |
| Work-in-process, September 30 | $ 30,914 | $ 11,000 | $ 27,924 | $69,838 |

At the same time, the Accountant has prepared a trial balance of the job cost ledger which indicates that the work-in-process at September 30 is almost $35,000 below the above figures — that is, the detailed listing of each job in process produces the following totals:

| Direct Material | $21,575 |
|---|---|
| Direct Labour | 9,375 |
| Factory Overhead | 4,300 |
| TOTAL | $35,250 |

The Vice-President, Finance is seriously concerned over these discrepancies and asks you to review the cost system.

Your scrutiny of the accounting records for the month discloses the following errors:

(1) Material issues totalled $223,575 but were journalized as $232,575.

(2) Freight-In amounting to $22,170 was incorrectly debited to Indirect Material in the Factory Overhead cost structure rather than being charged to Raw Material Stores.

(3) Direct Labour and Indirect Labour were each incorrectly charged with 50% of Office Salaries totalling $2,668.

(4) One machine on a total order for 15 was completed and billed during the month but Work-In-Process control account was not relieved for this shipment. The cost of this machine as shown by the job cost records was:

| | |
|---|---|
| Direct material | $339 |
| Direct labour | 291 |
| Factory overhead | 120 |
| | $750 |

You are also able to ascertain that these errors were not carried through to the detailed job cost records but were only reflected in the control accounts for the system.

Prepare a revised schedule of production showing the movement in work-in-process for the month after making the necessary adjustments to correct the errors that have come to light.

# THREE

## TYPES OF COST SYSTEMS

When talking about a *type* of cost system, we mean the mechanics by which per-unit costs are determined. As in the case of most generalizations, this one is also subject to qualification, but it does serve to emphasize the differences between two of the major types: job order cost systems and process cost systems.

The type of cost system used by any particular organization is basically a function of the nature of the business carried on. Thus, generally speaking, continuous or mass-production industries use process cost systems, while custom manufacturers that produce rather specialized products or manufacture to order use job order systems. At the same time, it is not inconceivable that the same company might employ both systems. For example, a furniture company may use a job order cost system for its line of quality wood furniture and a process cost system for its plastic auditorium chairs that are mass-produced on a standardized basis, a situation where the identification of individual items or lots produced ceases to be significant. Thus, while certain industries have come to be associated with a certain type of cost system in the past, the current trend towards diversification together with the dramatic changes in technology produced by automation, may be expected to have a significant impact on costing techniques in the future. An example of this is already evident in the development of what are termed *operational cost systems* that combine some of the features of both job cost and process cost systems. An operational cost system meets the requirements of assembly industries by making the operations through which the product passes the costing point rather than the whole order, or a complete department or cost centre. Hence, senior cost accountants and executives need to keep an open mind when it comes to deciding what approach is most suitable in any given circumstance.

However, it may be of some interest to know what industries have traditionally used which type of cost system in the past, although the author makes no warranties as to the completeness of the following list.

Businesses using
JOB ORDER COST SYSTEMS:

— aircraft manufacturers
— architects
— construction companies
— custom tailors
— engineers
— film producers
— foundries
— furniture manufacturers
— heavy machine tool
  manufacturers
— heavy machinery manufacturers
— machine shops
— plumbing and heating contractors
— printers
— service and repair shops
— ship builders
— structural steel fabricators

Businesses using
PROCESS COST SYSTEMS:

— bakeries
— breweries and distilleries
— bottlers of carbonated beverages
— brick manufacturers
— cement and lime mills
— chemical plants
— flour mills
— food canning and freezing plants
— glass manufacturers
— hosiery manufacturers
— laundries and dry cleaning plants
— logging and lumber mills
— meat packers
— mining companies
— oil refineries
— paint, varnish and lacquer
  manufacturers
— pharmaceutical manufacturers
— pipe manufacturers
— public utilities
— pulp and paper mills
— rubber processing plants
— sand and gravel quarries
— sugar refineries
— tanners and leather processors
— textile mills
— tin and iron mills

While it is not the aim of this book to make cost accountants out of non-financial executives, some knowledge of the mechanics of the various types of cost systems is necessary in order to gain a basic understanding of the function of Cost Accounting as a whole. Another reason for the descriptive outlines that follow is that we shall be drawing analogies later on between certain features of these traditional systems and some of the recent offshoots of cost accounting.

● JOB ORDER COST SYSTEMS

As the name suggests, this is a system for accumulating costs by separate and distinct jobs, orders or projects, as they are variously termed. At the elementary cost level, each element of cost: materials, labour and overhead, is posted to or entered on a job cost card for each separate job or order that is put into production. For control purposes, each job is assigned a number so that material requisitions and labour tickets, for example, can be easily coded and charged to the specific job for which the material was issued or the labour expended.

Each specific job may correspond to a customer's order or it may represent an internal order to replenish the company's stock of certain finished products or subassemblies. The cost of each item produced is determined by simply dividing the total cost on a completed job by the number of items on the order. Thus, if Job #8951, for example, covered an order for 15 cement mixers, and the final cost on completion of the job was $11,238.00, the cost per mixer would be $749.20.

The relationship between the individual jobs and the work-in-process inventory account or "bucket" is that the dollar balance in the latter should agree with the aggregate of the costs accumulated to date on all jobs in process at the end of any given accounting period. That is to say, while the individual job cost cards may be posted daily, it is generally not the practice to post the work-in-process control account on a daily basis; instead, material requisitions and labour tickets are accumulated in batches and once a week, once a month, or at the end of a four-week accounting period, they are posted in total to the control account in the general ledger or the cost ledger, depending upon the organization of the company's records. However, this statement is subject to qualification if EDP (electronic data processing) is used. Daily updating of all the records at every level within a system is more a feature of EDP than the "batch processing" approach that is common to most manual or partially mechanized systems.

To illustrate, let us assume that THE OLD-LINE MANUFACTURING COMPANY uses a job cost system, and that there were six jobs in process as at December 31, 19—. This being the case, we should be able to list the costs by elements on each open job at that date and agree the sum of these costs with the work-in-process control account:

| JOB NO. | MATERIALS | LABOUR | OVERHEAD | TOTAL |
|---------|-----------|--------|----------|-------|
| 8951 | $ 4,620 | $ 4,310 | $ 1,770 | $10,700 |
| 8952 | 3,500 | 3,260 | 1,340 | 8,100 |
| 8985 | 3,030 | 2,820 | 1,160 | 7,010 |
| 9001 | 10,300 | 9,610 | 3,950 | 23,860 |
| 9002 | 17,710 | 16,500 | 6,780 | 40,990 |
| 9003 | 2,840 | — | — | 2,840 |
| TOTALS | $42,000 | $36,500 | $15,000 | $93,500 |

A similar analysis may be prepared covering cost of goods sold for the period, if desired. In fact, some companies simply transfer the completed job cost cards to a separate file which then constitutes the finished goods ledger. This saves posting a separate record and transcribing, of necessity, a large amount of detailed information from the job cost card itself.

It is also the practice to prepare a cost estimate in advance in most businesses that utilize a job cost system, so that actual costs may be compared with the estimate when the job is complete. Such detailed costing by each order permits calculation of the profit (or loss) per job or project, and thus, hopefully, provides a basis for better estimating or more accurate quotations to customers in the future.

One of the disadvantages of a job order cost system is that it is generally expensive to maintain. Thus, if a large number of jobs are in process at any given date, one can easily visualize the amount of clerical time and effort involved in making the detailed entries on each one of several hundred or even several thousand individual job cost cards. Under these circumstances, then, some degree of mechanization of procedures is clearly indicated if the cost of cost-finding is to be kept at a reasonable level.

## • PROCESS COST SYSTEMS

In this type of cost system, the approach is to average department costs over department outputs. It assumes that the processes performed in each department are identical or virtually the same for all the materials processed, and that a homogeneous product is produced.

Under these circumstances, we are referring to *direct* or *productive* departments in which actual production of some tangible product occurs. There are other types of departments known as *indirect* or *service* departments whose main function is to provide for the systematic accumulation of overhead costs. This distinction between direct and indirect departments also applies under a job order cost system but is of less significance when the individual order is the costing point rather than an entire department.

Some students like to think of a direct department under process cost conditions as simply a large job order to which the elements of cost are posted in the same manner as to an individual job under a job order cost system. This is theoretically correct subject to the qualification that a direct department under a process cost system is seldom if ever closed out. By contrast, a job order, when the number of units specified by the order has been completed and transferred to finished goods, is considered to be closed and ceases to be a costing point. But there are usually some units in a more or less incomplete state left in a direct department at the end of a month or other accounting period, and the process is a continuous one. Hence, if a direct department is thought of as a job order, it must be visualized as an open-ended one. Probably a more precise analogy is to picture a direct department under a process cost system as a specific work-in-process bucket that happens to be classified according to the process carried on in the department rather than simply by the major elements of cost, as was illustrated in Figure 6.

In order to develop unit costs, it is necessary to allocate the total costs for the period over all units that enter into the process, whether complete or incomplete. In other words, it is necessary to determine the *effective production* for the period (also termed *equivalent production* or *equivalent performance*), which simply means that the opening and closing inventories, if any, must be stated in terms of the equivalent finished units they represent. It is the practice, generally, to determine the effective production separately for each element of cost: materials, labour and overhead. It often happens that all the material is issued at the beginning of a process so that at the end of the cost period, the units still incomplete are nevertheless 100% complete as regards their material content. However, if materials, labour and overhead are applied uniformly throughout the process, a calculation of effective production for the process as a whole will produce satisfactory unit costs. For the sake of simplicity in the illustration which follows, this assumption is made.

In order to demonstrate the flexibility of our model enterprise (or of Cost Accounting itself) let us change the product produced from construction equipment to moulded plastic chairs. This type of product lends itself readily to a simple process cost system with only two direct departments, Moulding and Assembly. In the first department, the plastic chair seats and backs are formed according to a standard pattern; in the second department, the seat and back units are bolted onto metal frames. As a refinement, you can also assume that the chair forms and metal bases are spray-painted in matching colours in order to provide some variety in the product, but otherwise, no further operations are required prior to shipment to customers.

The analysis by direct department of the aggregate costs previously developed is assumed to be as follows:

| DOLLAR OUTLAYS: | MOULDING DEPT. | ASSEMBLY DEPT. | TOTAL | FINISHED GOODS |
|---|---|---|---|---|
| Work-in-process, beginning | $ 19,375 | $ 80,625 | $ 100,000 | |
| Materials issued | 540,625 | 309,375 | 850,000 | |
| Direct labour applied | 135,000 | 600,000 | 735,000 | |
| Overhead applied | 58,000 | 257,500 | 315,500 | |
| | $753,000 | $1,247,500 | $2,000,500 | |
| Transferred to Assembly Department | (696,900) | 696,900 | — | |
| | | $1,944,400 | | |
| Transferred to Finished Goods | — | (1,907,000) | (1,907,000) | $1,907,000 |
| Work-in-process, end | $ 56,100 | $ 37,400 | $ 93,500 | |

| UNITS OF PRODUCT: | MOULDING DEPT. | ASSEMBLY DEPT. |
|---|---|---|
| Work-in-process, beginning: | | |
| 12,000 units | | |
| 50% complete | 6,000 | |
| 16,125 units | | |
| ⅔ complete | | 10,750 |
| Put into production | 245,000 | — |
| | ............................... | |
| Units completed and transferred out | 232,300 | 238,375 |
| Work-in-process, end: | | |
| 23,375 units | | |
| 80% complete | 18,700 | |
| 9,350 units | | |
| 50% complete | — | 4,675 |
| | 251,000 | 243,050 |
| Unit Costs | $    3.00 | $    8.00 |

The unit costs are computed in this example using the "unit costs of the period" formula, viz.,

$$\frac{\text{Cost of inventory, beginning} + \text{Current outlays for the period}}{\text{Number of units completed} + \text{Effective production in inventory, end}} = \text{Unit Costs of the Period}$$

In the case of the Moulding Department, the calculations are:

$$\frac{\$19,375 + \$733,625}{232,300 + 18,700} = \frac{\$753,000}{251,000}$$
$$= \$3.00 \text{ per unit.}$$

In the case of the Assembly Department, the calculations are:

$$\frac{\$80,625 + \$1,863,775}{238,375 + 4,675} = \frac{\$1,944,400}{243,050}$$
$$= \$8.00 \text{ per unit.}$$

When the "unit costs of the period" method is used, the period-end inventories and the transfers to the next department or to finished goods, as the case may be, are costed at the same per unit cost:

| | MOULDING DEPT. | ASSEMBLY DEPT. | FINISHED GOODS |
|---|---|---|---|
| Work-in-process, end: | | | |
| 18,700 x $3.00 | $    56,100 | | |
| 4,675 x $8.00 | — | $    37,400 | |
| Units completed and transferred out: | | | |
| 232,300 x $3.00 | (696,900) | 696,900 | |
| 238,375 x $8.00 | — | (1,907,000) | $1,907,000 |

The preceding simple formula is generally considered to be appropriate when the inventories of work-in-process are not large in relation to the outlays for the period and when the variations in costs from period to period are not too significant.

A more sophisticated approach, termed the "unit costs of the process" method, excludes the influence of the costs in the beginning inventory in developing a current process unit cost. The latter is then used to value the ending inventory. The transfers to the next department or to finished goods are then valued at the residual cost, which is a blend of current outlays and the costs in the opening inventory. The resulting unit costs produced by this method are almost identical with those produced by the simpler "unit costs of the period" method. However, the mechanics should be understood, since the use of this more elaborate formula is rather widespread, viz.,

$$\frac{\text{Outlays for the period}}{\begin{array}{c}\text{Portion of beginning} \\ \text{inventory completed} \\ \text{in current period}\end{array} + \begin{array}{c}\text{Units started} \\ \text{and finished}\end{array} + \begin{array}{c}\text{Equivalent production} \\ \text{in inventory, end}\end{array}} = \begin{array}{c}\text{Unit} \\ \text{Costs} \\ \text{of the} \\ \text{Process}\end{array}$$

Considering first the Moulding Department, the calculations are as follows:

| | | | |
|---|---|---:|---:|
| Outlays for the period, excluding costs in Beginning inventory ($753,000 — $19,375) | | | $733,625 (A) |
| Equivalent production involved in completion of opening inventory, 50% × 12,000 | | | 6,000 |
| Units started | | 245,000 | |
| *Less* units in closing inventory | | 23,375 | 221,625 |
| Equivalent production in closing inventory, 80% × 23,375 | | | 18,700 |
| | | | 246,325 (B) |
| Unit costs of the process (A/B) | | | $ 2.9783 |
| Valuation of closing inventory, 18,700 × $2.9783 | | | $ 55,694 |

Having arrived at a valuation for the closing inventory, sufficient information is now available to determine the cost of the transfers to the next department.

| | UNITS | UNIT COSTS | DOLLARS |
|---|---:|---:|---:|
| Opening inventory | 6,000 | $3.2292 | $   19,375 |
| Put into production | 245,000 | 2.9944 | 733,625 |
| | 251,000 | 3.0000 | $ 753,000 |
| Closing inventory | 18,700 | 2.9783 | 55,694 |
| Transferred to Assembly Department | 232,300 | $3.0017 | $ 697,306 |

In the same fashion, calculations for the Assembly Department are:

Outlays for the period, excluding costs
  in the opening inventory:

| | |
|---|---:|
| Materials issued | $ 309,375 |
| Direct labour applied | 600,000 |
| Overhead applied | 257,500 |
| | $1,166,875 |
| Transferred from Moulding Department (as above) | 697,306 |
| TOTAL | $1,864,181 (A) |

| | | |
|---|---:|---:|
| Equivalent production involved in completion of opening inventory, ⅓ × 16,125 | | 5,375 |
| Units started | 232,300 | |
| *Less* units in closing inventory | 9,350 | 222,950 |
| Equivalent production in closing inventory, 50% × 9,350 | | 4,675 |
| | | 233,000 (B) |

| | |
|---|---:|
| Unit costs of the process (A/B) | $ 7.9990 |
| Valuation of closing inventory, 4,675 × $7.9990 | $ 37,395 |

The transfers to finished goods may now be costed:

| | UNITS | UNIT COSTS | DOLLARS |
|---|---:|---:|---:|
| Opening inventory | 10,750 | $7.5000 | $ 80,625 |
| Put into production (see (A) above) | 232,300 | 8.0250 | 1,864,181 |
| | 243,050 | 8.0017 | $1,944,806 |
| Closing inventory | 4,675 | 7.9990 | 37,395 |
| Transferred to Finished Goods | 238,375 | 8.0017 | $1,907,411 |

There have been two rather subtle assumptions implicit in these calculations that would not be entirely obvious at first glance even to an experienced cost accountant. That is, the assumption of "first-in — first-out" was made as regards the flow of units through each department, and the cost of any units spoiled or otherwise lost in the process was ignored, or more precisely, this hidden cost was not sorted out but was simply allowed to increase the average cost of the remaining good units. Is this the correct approach? The answer depends on how significant spoilage, shrinkage, or scrap is in the process. In this case, it is relatively minor if we take the trouble to account for the total number of units involved from the beginning to the end of the period.

| MOULDING DEPARTMENT: | | TOTAL UNITS | % COMPLETE |
|---|---:|---:|---:|
| Inventory, beginning | | 12,000 | 50% |
| Put into production | | 245,000 | |
| | | 257,000 | |
| Spoiled units | 1,325 | | |
| Transferred to Assembly Department | 232,300 | 233,625 | |
| Inventory, end | | 23,375 | 80% |

| ASSEMBLY DEPARTMENT: | | TOTAL UNITS | % COMPLETE |
|---|---|---|---|
| Inventory, beginning | | 16,125 | 2/3 |
| Transferred from Moulding Department | | 232,300 | |
| | | 248,425 | |
| Spoiled units | 700 | | |
| Transferred to Finished Goods | 238,375 | 239,075 | |
| Inventory, end | | 9,350 | 50% |

When there are inventories of work-in-process at the end of the account-ing period, the accuracy of the costing is obviously dependent upon the tally or measurement of the units in process and the estimate of the state of completion of these units. If either or both these factors are inaccurate, the unit costs produced will not be reliable indicators of average cost, nor useful as control tools to measure efficiency.

The preceding examples have served to illustrate the mechanics of a process cost system under rather simple conditions. It should be understood that considerably greater complexity will be found in specific industries, depending upon the characteristics of the manufacturing process carried on.

### • STANDARD COST SYSTEMS

A rather serious limitation of the two types of costs systems previously outlined is that they only provide information covering product costs *after* the completion of the work involved (when a job order is complete, for example) or at the close of the accounting period (when the departmental process costs have been determined). While such *historical cost* systems, as they are termed, are usually a vast improvement over a general accounting system in a manufacturing environment, insofar as they shorten the period that management has to wait for information needed to plan and control operations, a natural evolutionary step is the provision of more timely and reliable control data in the form of *standard costs*. Standard costs, as the name implies, are predetermined costs designed to provide a measure against which actual performance may be gauged. Among the more obvious advan-tages of standard costs are the following:

(1) Standard costs provide a yardstick or basis for comparison that historical costs lack.
(2) Use is made of the "principle of exceptions" whereby attention is focussed on variances from standard thus eliminating the laborious and often unsatisfactory process of comparing the operating results of one period with those of another in order to detect items requiring attention.
(3) Standard costs produce a figure for operating costs in advance

thereby providing a basis for setting prices, making quotations, valuing inventories, and so forth.

(4) Clerical labour and expense in the cost department is generally reduced — for example, the subsidiary perpetual stock records for direct materials and finished products need only be kept in quantities which can be extended at standard prices as the occasion demands; it is not necessary to extend individual stock requisitions; entries on individual cost sheets are not required.

This saving in clerical time and effort can (hopefully) be expended in producing more useful cost information, making special cost studies, etc.

(5) Standard costs generally facilitate the introduction and use of complete budgetary controls.

Setting standard costs involves the application of the related disciplines of industrial engineering and cost accounting. Thus, when standard costs are used, they should be regarded as *true costs* and actual costs are of interest only insofar as they measure deviations or variances from these predetermined norms. If line management can argue that variances from the standard costs are the result of incorrect or inaccurate standards having been set, then, of course, the standards are valueless.[1] Hence the necessity for precision in setting the standards so that such challenges can be avoided, and management can have confidence in the reliability of the standards as measures of attainable performance under prevailing conditions.

## Direct Material Standards

The standards for this element of cost involve detail specifications of the kind, quantity and price of each part or product that enters into the production process. In order to determine price standards, it is necessary to decide upon the economical lot run of each type of product that is to be produced at a given time — this is where the role of the industrial engineer becomes important. The information supplied by this engineering study provides the necessary data to the purchasing department so that stocks of materials may be adjusted to take advantage of quantity discounts or to reduce carrying charges on inventories to a minimum. Even in a custom shop that manufactures to customers' specifications, it is usually possible to use similar materials for the majority of special orders so that no serious problems are involved in stocking nonstandard parts.

As a certain amount of waste or spoilage is usually inherent in every process, material standards set should include a reasonable allowance for this.

## Direct Labour Standards

Setting labour standards is most satisfactorily achieved by the use of time and motion studies or the application of predetermined standards such as are developed by MTM.[2]

An alternative procedure is to average past performance, although this approach is usually open to question, since working conditions are seldom static and changes in production methods may have taken place during the period under study.

Labour rate standards involve a classification of the work force into grades and the setting of standard rates of pay for each grade. Here, as in the case of time standards, a scientific study should first be made of the whole field of employee compensation in order to set rates which fairly represent the job relative to others in the organization. After labour has been graded, specifications are set indicating the grade of labour to be used for each operation performed and the standard time allowance therefor.

### Overhead Standards

Standards for overhead or manufacturing expense are generally based on "flexible budgets" or schedules of expenses by department at each level of activity. For each rise or fall in activity, the amount of additional expense allowable or the normal reduction in expense is specified.

The determination of overhead standards involves consideration of what constitutes normal productive capacity in the plant. Certain overhead expenses are fixed, some are semivariable, and others are completely variable at different levels of activity. This could obviously cause considerable variation in unit costs if overhead were charged to the product on an actual basis.

In setting standard overhead rates for the purpose of applying manufacturing expense to each unit of product produced, it is advisable to use a standard based on normal expected productive capacity. Having designated this level as "normal" and set rates that will absorb 100% of the fixed overhead in the product at this level, the effect of variations in activity may be measured by volume variances (also termed *activity* or *capacity* variances).

As the last statement demonstrates, there is an unfortunate lack of standardization in the terminology of Cost Accounting. It is not that one cost accountant cannot understand the dialect of another, but the layman or nonfinance-oriented executive has no way of knowing that a lot of the terms in Cost Accounting are substitutes for one another or mean substantially the same thing. For example, the terms "overhead" or "factory overhead" or "factory overhead expenses" have been used interchangeably so far to designate the whole group of costs that make up the factory (mill, plant, works, etc.) indirect expenses in a manufacturing business. It may come as somewhat of a shock to the reader at this point to learn that there are more than a dozen terms in fairly common usage to label this cost structure — namely:

Burden

Factory Burden
Factory Expense
Factory Overhead
Factory Service
Factory Service Expense

Indirect Cost
Indirect Expense

Manufacturing Burden
Manufacturing Expense
Manufacturing Overhead

Overhead

Plant Burden
Plant Expense
Plant Overhead

Works Expense
Works Overhead

The same phenomenon applies to the variances developed by a standard cost system. Unfortunately, there can be no solution to this problem until the various professional associations — to which accountants in general and cost accountants in particular belong — get together and decide to cooperate in the development of common terminology. In the interim, the writer has used what seem to be the most familiar or generally accepted terms in this and other chapters, without claiming the sanction of any particular association of cost accountants or the endorsement of any respected textbook author.

### Variances from Standard

Although it is possible to control performance in a factory within reasonably close limits, inevitably there are going to be some deviations between the actual costs incurred and the standards set. Cost Accounting generally analyzes these deviations into seven *variances* as shown in Figure 9. In this table, the term "difference" has been used consistently to indicate the variance involved without specifying whether it is plus or minus. In accounting terminology, the difference between the first and second operand (the variance) would be a debit or credit — a debit or positive result indicating an unfavourable variance, and a credit or negative difference denoting a favourable variance.

The mechanics of calculating these variances is considered in the next chapter dealing with costs at the elementary level. At this point, it is

## Figure 9.

### THE SEVEN COMMON VARIANCES

| NAME OF VARIANCE | HOW CALCULATED |
| --- | --- |
| Direct Material Price Variance | — Difference between (1) actual direct material purchased at actual cost and (2) standard cost for the actual quantity purchased.* |
| Direct Material Usage Variance | — Difference between (1) actual quantity issued or transferred to work-in-process and (2) standard quantity, both being priced or costed at standard. |
| Direct Labour Rate Variance | — Difference between (1) actual hours worked at actual rates and (2) actual hours extended at standard rates. |
| Direct Labour Efficiency Variance | — Difference between (1) actual hours applied to work-in-process at standard rates and (2) standard hours at standard rates. |
| Overhead Spending Variance | — Difference between (1) actual overhead expense for the period and (2) allowed budget for the actual hours worked. |
| Overhead Efficiency Variance | — Difference between (1) actual hours worked at standard rates and (2) standard hours in the product at standard rates. |
| Overhead Volume Variance | — Difference between (1) allowed budget for the actual hours worked and (2) actual hours at standard rates. |

*Some businesses do not identify the price variance until material is issued from stores. However, there are several advantages to keeping Stores or Raw Materials Inventory Account at standard, so that the point of purchase is the preferred stage for sorting out this variance.

sufficient to note that such variances are an important feature of a standard cost system. They may or may not influence the format of the operating statement. Thus, referring back to Figure 8, the amount $1,898,500 representing "Cost of Goods Sold" might have been made up of a standard cost of goods sold amount plus or minus a number of variances, see Figure 10.

The general practice is to write off such variances to cost of sales during the year (as shown), although some accountants are in favour of distributing the variances over inventory and cost of goods sold in order that both items may be shown at actual cost in the financial statements. Another school of thought recommends that they (the variances) be carried as deferred credits, if favourable or credit balances, and as deferred charges, if unfavourable or debit balances. In any case, the variances would probably only appear in the management reports used for internal control purposes, and not in the published financial reports released to outsiders. The general

## Figure 10.

THE OLD-LINE MANUFACTURING COMPANY
COST OF GOODS SOLD
Year ended December 31, 19—

Cost of Goods Sold at standard:

| | | |
|---|---|---|
| Direct Material | | $  839,000 |
| Direct Labour | | 682,550 |
| Overhead | | 368,450 |
| | | $1,890,000 |

*Add* Variances from standard cost incurred during the year:

| | | |
|---|---|---|
| Direct Material Price Variances | ($16,200) | |
| Direct Material Usage Variances | 26,700 | 10,500 |
| Direct Labour Rate Variances | $36,750 | |
| Direct Labour Efficiency Variances | 14,700 | 51,450 |
| Overhead Spending Variances | ($36,840) | |
| Overhead Efficiency Variances | 6,280 | |
| Overhead Volume Variances | (22,890) | (53,450) |
| Cost of Goods Sold at actual | | $1,898,500 |

public, it is felt, does not possess the degree of sophistication necessary to understand the significance of variances. There is perhaps some truth in this reasoning, since the absolute amounts can appear rather startling to a non-accountant even when related to the aggregate standard cost elements to which they pertain.

• REFERENCES

1. This refers to what is more precisely described as *current standards,* or standards that are intended to be representative of what costs should actually be under prevailing conditions. There are other types of standards, such as *basic standards* which are designed to be used more as a point of reference or base for computing indices that measure trends or changes since the base was established. It is not proposed to debate the usefulness of these other types of standards, and all references to standard costs in this and other chapters apply only to *current standards.*

2. MTM is the abbreviation for Methods-Time Measurement, a pre-determined motion time system that uses TMU's (time measurement units) each one of which represents 1/100,000 of an hour. The authors

of the technique are Maynard, Stegemerten and Schwab who first published their findings under the title, *Methods-Time Measurement,* McGraw-Hill Book Company, Inc., New York, 1948. At this date, there is a considerable body of knowledge surrounding the use of MTM, and information concerning its application in a particular industry may be obtained from a large number of consulting firms or direct from the "MTM Association for Standards and Research," 9 - 10 Saddle River Road, Fair Lawn, New Jersey, 07410, USA.

● QUESTIONS AND CASE PROBLEMS

3.01 Indicate whether you would expect to find a Job Order Cost System or a Process Cost System in the following enterprises:

(a) The Jarvis Aircraft Corporation

(b) Hagersville Hand Laundry

(c) Montréal Tool & Die Inc.

(d) Les Entrepreneurs de Plomberie Enrg.

(e) Baffinland Mining & Refining Co. Ltd.

(f) La Compagnie des Meubles Modernes Ltée.

3.02 When is it appropriate to use the simpler "unit costs of the period" method rather than the "unit costs of the process" method in a process cost system?

3.03 What happens to the cost of spoiled units in a process cost system?

3.04 Explain the difference between an historical cost system and a standard cost system.

3.05 State the benefits that may be expected to accrue from the use of a standard cost system.

3.06 Can a cost accountant install a standard cost system alone and unaided?

3.07 How are standards set for (a) direct material, (b) direct labour, and (c) overhead?

3.08 State the variances that are commonly developed by a standard cost system.

3.09 What is a useful rule for determining whether a variance is favourable or unfavourable?

3.10 A custom machine knife manufacturer produces planer knives for

17 different machines utilized by various lumber mills throughout the province. Does this mean that the machine knife manufacturer cannot make use of cost standards?

3.11    If the variances from standard cost are not written off to Cost of Goods Sold, what other ways are there to deal with them in the accounts and financial statements of a business?

3.12    Restructure the Cost of Goods Sold schedule (Figure 10) so that only the actual total cost figures for direct material, direct labour and overhead are shown.

3.13    (a) Calculate the percentage ratio of standard to actual cost for each of the major cost elements, using the data in 3.12 above. Your answer should be calculated to four decimal places (or 1/10,000 of 1%).

   (b) Assuming the variances in Figure 10. are not to be written off entirely to cost of goods sold but are to be prorated over work-in-process, finished goods and cost of goods sold, calculate the revised amount for "cost of goods sold, actual" to the nearest $100 (refer to the analysis of work-in-process and finished goods in Chapter 2 to develop your answer).

   (c) Determine the amount by which "cost of goods sold, actual" as calculated in (b) above is less than "cost of goods sold, actual" in Figure 10., and the additional income taxes payable by THE OLD LINE MANUFACTURING COMPANY as a result of the decision to prorate the variances over inventories and cost of goods sold. Assume a tax rate of 52% applies.

3.14    KINCARDINE MILLWORK LIMITED makes quotations on the basis of an allowance for mill overhead of 100% of direct labour and a 25% mark-up applied to mill cost for selling expense and profit.

Calculate what the selling price should be, to the nearest $10, for the following orders:

|  |  | Material | Direct Labour |
|---|---|---|---|
| 3841 | Stairs, oak treads, fir risers | $347.22 | $147.08 |
| 3842 | Window stool, oak | 51.48 | 18.66 |
| 3843 | Laminated tops, glued | 30.45 | 9.06 |
| 3844 | Laminated tops, bolted | 144.38 | 48.34 |

3.15    LES VOITURES ETRANGERES LTEE. imports foreign cars at a basic price of 7.500 francs per vehicle (7,500 French francs) payable against a sight draft at Montréal. During the month of May,

30 cars were unloaded at the docks in Montréal. Federal duty and sales taxes are payable at an effective rate of 28.8% of the Canadian equivalent of invoiced value and a provincial sales tax of 8% applies to the "landed cost" which includes federal duty and sales taxes. Cartage from the docks to the garage of LES VOITURES amounts to $14.40 per vehicle. New car servicing of $20.67 per unit is required before the vehicles are ready for demonstration or sale.

The dealer had no cars in stock prior to this shipment, but sold 10 units at $2,542.50 each prior to May 31.

The conversion rate at the date of clearance through customs was franc = $0.1916 CDN.

Calculate the Sales, Cost of Goods and Gross Margin realized by LES VOITURES for the month, and the per-unit and total cost of the month-end inventory of new cars on hand. (Round off all calculations to the nearest dollar.)

3.16 **THE CHLORO CHEMICAL COMPANY** produces a liquid cleanser which requires only two processes, mixing and bottling. Two basic materials are involved: a solvent issued to the Mixing Department and plastic containers (bottles) used in the Bottling Department.

Total materials issued during the month of August were:

```
Solvent    —   200,000 gallons @ $0.24
Containers — 2,740,000 bottles @ $0.02
```

Each gallon of solvent should, in the absence of shrinkage, produce 2 cases of cleanser, each case containing 6 bottles. The case is thus the basic unit of measurement in each department.

According to the Company's records, work-in-process inventories at August 1 were as follows:

| | | | % COMPLETE | COST |
|---|---|---|---|---|
| Mixing | — material | 24,000 cases | 100% | $ 2,640 |
| | — labour | | 50% | 3,480 |
| | — overhead | | 50% | 840 |
| Bottling | — material | 40,000 cases | 100% | $25,200 |
| | — labour | | 30% | 2,760 |
| | — overhead | | 30% | 480 |

Labour and overhead for the month of August were charged as follows:

| | MIXING | BOTTLING |
|---|---|---|
| labour | $119,280 | $92,928 |
| overhead | 31,808 | 19,360 |

The inventories of work-in-process at August 31st have been tallied but not costed:

|  |  |  | % COMPLETE |
|---|---|---|---|
| Mixing | — material | 36,000 cases | 100% |
|  | — labour |  | 60% |
|  | — overhead |  | 60% |
| Bottling | — material | 48,000 cases | 100% |
|  | — labour |  | 40% |
|  | — overhead |  | 40% |

The equivalent of 388,000 cases of cleanser was transferred to the Bottling Department during the month, and 380,000 cases of bottled cleanser were transferred to the finished goods warehouse.

Prepare schedules showing how the completed production and month-end inventories are valued, and the unit costs developed in each department for each element of cost: materials, labour and overhead (treat the transfers from one department to another as a material cost in the receiving department).

Make the calculations and prepare the relevant schedules
using  (a) the "unit costs of the process method,"
  and  (b) the "unit costs of the period" method.
Unit cost calculations need not be carried beyond four decimal places.
     (c) Calculate the apparent loss in bottles for the month.
        Is this loss or shrinkage significant?

# FOUR

## THE ELEMENTS OF COST

Among the important attributes of Cost Accounting is a more elaborate and scientific analysis of outlays than is contemplated by a general accounting system. As a result, certain rather complex subsystems are generally an integral part of a cost system to account for and control each element of cost through the input and output stages until the final resting place in a cost structure is reached. Of necessity, these subsystems are concerned with the recording and classification of elementary costs at the lowest level of analysis within the overall system — an item of material issued, a fraction of an hour's labour, or an expense transaction charged to an overhead account.

- DIRECT MATERIAL

In Figure 5, raw materials were shown to be one of the three major inputs to work-in-process. However, this was somewhat of an over-simplification since not *all* raw materials issued end up in work-in-process except in the simplest types of operations. More often such issues are distributed to a number of expense or cost accounts in various structures as well, although the greater part usually does go to work-in-process. This multiple distribution of the issues from raw material stores is illustrated in Figure 11.

The important features of the subsystem controlling materials are as follows:

(1) All purchases of material and supplies are charged initially to an inventory account which generally bears the label RAW MATERIALS or STORES.

(2) Issues or transfers out are classified or coded as to their ultimate use.

(3) Only *direct material* is charged to WORK-IN-PROCESS, MATERIAL.

**Figure 11.**

## THE DISTRIBUTION OF MATERIAL ISSUES

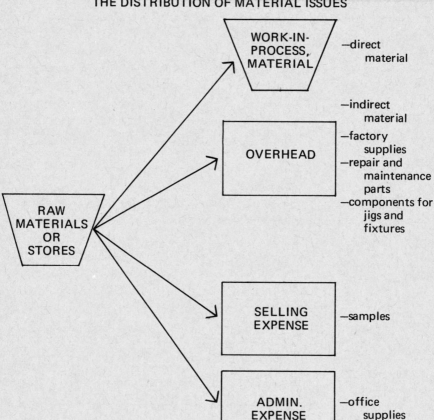

The distinction between direct and indirect material is rather important. By definition, direct material (a) must constitute a sufficiently important element to be measurable in the final product, and (b) must be directly chargeable to a production order or manufacturing process. For example, thread in the garment industry meets the second test but its cost is so slight per garment produced that it is not practical to account for its usage. Hence, it is classified as an indirect material as a matter of convenience.

The fact that accounting control is established over all purchases of tangible items by charging such items to an account labelled "stores" also implies that there shall be physical control over the items as they are received. In fact, this is the standard practice in any business that uses an integrated cost system. That is, all receipts of materials and supplies are placed — usually in bins or on shelves or racks — in a fenced-off area under the control and custody of a Storekeeper. Issues from the stockroom are then made only upon the authority of a properly approved materials requisition, one of the numerous pieces of paper or unit records required to maintain the inventory control system. To describe in detail the methods and procedures involved in handling such records would require an entire book in itself. However, the nonfinancial executive should at least be aware of the function that some of the more important forms serve in maintaining a cost system, i.e.,

*purchase requisition* — A request to the purchasing department to buy materials or supplies, either for stock or for a specific job or production order.

*purchase order* — The formal contract with the vendor to supply the specified items in accordance with the terms (including the price) stated in the purchase order.

*receiving report* — A list of the items actually received from the vendor prepared by the receiver. Often a copy of the purchase order with the quantities blanked out serves as a receiving report. This latter practice is preferable since it compels the receiver(s) to actually count, weigh, or otherwise measure the incoming items.

*purchase invoice* — The account rendered for the items supplied by the vendor. In a standard cost system, the standard cost and the price variance are generally entered on the face of the invoice (or a copy) in order to establish the proper accounting distribution on the source document inself.

*stores ledger* — A record, covering each individual item of material or supplies maintained in the stockroom, showing receipts, issues, and the balance on hand. Receipts are posted from receiving reports and issues are entered from the materials requisitions. This record may be maintained in quantities only or in both quantities and dollars.

*materials requisition* — A voucher authorizing the stockkeeper to issue certain specified items for use in the factory or elsewhere. Space for the account to be charged and/or the job order is usually an integral part of this form for obvious reasons. Note that *credit requisitions* are also used to provide for negative issues or returns to stores.

*materials requisition* — A listing of all materials issued for a given period
*journal*                showing the dollar distribution to materials-in-pro-
                         cess, overhead and any other accounts affected;
                         also termed a requisition record, a summary of
                         material requisitions, and a materials distribution
                         journal.

The last-noted form raises the question of how the issues from stores are
to be valued. At least five methods are in fairly common use.

1. Actual cost of specific items.
2. First-in — first-out (FIFO).
3. Average cost.
4. Last-in — first-out (LIFO).
5. Standard cost.

In general, the first method would only be used by manufacturers of
custom products, and then only in connection with special purchases
ordered for a specific job or production order.

The average cost method has the advantage of simplicity, the unit price
for issues being calculated by dividing the quantity on hand into the dollar
balance at any given date.

LIFO has increased in popularity during the last two decades or so,
especially in those jurisdictions where it is now recognized by the taxing
authorities as an acceptable method for inventory valuation in arriving at
taxable income. Its proponents also claim that it results in a better matching
of costs against revenues especially in those industries where selling prices
are quite sensitive to changes in replacement or reproductive cost. However, this question belongs to the field of accounting theory and is one that
would require an entire volume to explore in depth. Suffice it to say that
business managers who are concerned with the results from a cost system
should be aware of what costing method is employed in valuing the periodic
inventories of the business, and how well the method succeeds in matching
current costs with current sales.

When the standard cost method is used, it is a relatively simple procedure
to cost material requisitions at standard, and generally requires less work
than the alternative procedures under an actual cost system. Partially
offsetting this is the additional work of costing the purchase invoices at
standard. On the other hand, if price variances are sorted out at the time
of receipt of the materials, a current indicator is provided showing the
trend of variances. Analysis can then be employed to ascertain whether the
variances are simply the result of changes in price levels since the standards
were set, or poor purchasing practices — e.g., buying from non-approved
suppliers, failure to observe the economic lot size on orders, and so forth.

The Direct Material Price Variance was defined in Chapter 3 as the difference between actual and standard cost of the actual quantity purchased. Thus, assuming that THE OLD-LINE MANUFACTURING COMPANY purchased 150,000 pounds of plastic for use in the manufacture of its line of auditorium chairs at $55.50 per cwt. and the standard cost had been established at $56.00 per cwt., a favourable price variance would be realized — viz., 1,500 cwt. @ 50¢, or $750.00 CR.

PROOF:  Actual cost    — 1,500 cwt. @ $55.50 = $83,250.00
        Standard cost — 1,500 cwt. @ $56.00 =  84,000.00
        Direct Material Price Variance _____   ($750.00)

The Direct Material Usage Variance is usually recorded at the point of transfer to work-in-process, although in point of time this may not be until the completion of a specific job or the end of an accounting period when information is available to show whether or not actual material used was in excess of or less than the standard quantity allowed for the finished product produced.

To return to the example of THE OLD-LINE MANUFACTURING COMPANY, if the production for the month was 20,300 chairs with 5 pounds of plastic being the standard allowance per chair, the amount of plastic consumed during the period should have been 20,300 × 5 lbs., or 101,500 lbs. If the actual usage was 102,100 lbs., we can conclude that a Direct Material Usage Variance of 600 lbs. has occurred (in this case, an unfavourable or debit variance), or 6 cwt. @ $56.00 = $336.00 DR.

PROOF:  Actual quantity consumed — 1,021 cwt. @ $56.00 = $57,176.00
        Standard quantity allowed — 1,015 cwt. @ $56.00 =  56,840.00
        Direct Material Usage Variance _____   $  336.00

Finally, the point should not be overlooked that the unit cost usually includes a number of elements in addition to the basic invoice cost such as freight and cartage inwards, duty and excise tax in the case of imported items, and what is often termed *material overhead*. The latter represents the cost of material handling in or around the factory (from the receiving area to the storeroom, and from the storeroom to the processing area), the cost of keeping the stores ledger, and even the clerical and administrative costs associated with the purchasing, receiving, and issuing functions. Notwithstanding the apparent difficulty of calculating accurate unit costs for such elements, they are logically as much a part of the total outlay involved in rendering the material available for use on the factory floor as the actual purchase cost paid to the vendor.

● DIRECT LABOUR

As in the case of materials, a distinction is made between direct and indirect cost when accounting for labour under virtually all types of cost systems.

Direct labour is usually defined as that portion of labour cost which can be applied specifically to units of product or to a process which involves the direct production of units of product. Indirect labour is the residual pool of labour costs.

With the advent of automated factories, the distinction between direct and indirect labour has become somewhat blurred. Is the worker who simply pushes buttons and watches dials engaged in direct labour? Orthodox theory suggests that he is. In other words, if a worker is simply tending a productive machine, his labour is considered to be as direct as that of a worker producing a product by hand. But the question becomes rather academic in the case of a fully automated department; under these circumstances, labour, whether direct or indirect, tends to be a relatively minor proportion of the total production costs. Hence, whether labour is applied directly to the job or process or indirectly as part of the overhead of the department on (say) a machine-hour basis, the results in terms of the total per-unit cost of the product will probably be identical.

However, the use of the rather invidious term "non-productive labour" tends to be misleading when referring to any labour not classified as direct. A wide variety of services are required in any manufacturing business simply to keep the factory operating. Without these support services, the machines engaged in turning out the finished products of the enterprise would soon cease to run.

Each plant has its own requirements for labour analysis but the following list is indicative of the many services that are an essential feature of any manufacturing environment: [1]

- supervision (salaried)
- supervision (hourly)
- clerical
- sweeping and cleaning
- watchmen and guards
- inspection
- reworking
- set-ups
- lost time
- repairs to machinery
- repairs to buildings
- experimental
- boxing and loading
- handling production materials
- overtime premiums
- training

The timekeeping and payroll procedures of manufacturing companies tend to be as complex as those within the subsystem that controls materials.

Among the numerous forms used, the following are perhaps most relevant to the cost system:

*time card* — A record of the total time spent on a daily or shift basis. As a rule, the employee's time of arrival at the factory and his time of departure are punched on the card by means of a time-recording clock. Hence, this record is also called a clock card, an attendance card or an in-and-out card.

*time ticket* — Also known as a labour ticket or unit labour cost ticket, this record shows how the worker's time was spent in contrast to the time card which is simply a record of the total time worked. A separate time ticket is usually generated for every job worked on or each operation performed. While the time card is the primary record for preparation of the payroll (unless a piece work or incentive system is in effect), the time ticket provides the basis for the labour distribution summary. Needless to say, both records should balance for any given period, day or week. If time is recorded in very small increments on the time ticket (say, 1/100 of an hour), there is bound to be small differences between the time card and the total time shown by the labour tickets for the day. In such cases it is usual to round off the time ticket hours to some predetermined interval such as a quarter of an hour or pool all such "unapplied time" by departments in an appropriate overhead account.

*labour distribution* — A summary of the labour cost for the period by job order number or by direct departments, in the case of direct labour, and by department and account classification (supervision, clerical, clean-up labour, etc.) in the case of indirect labour. The total labour cost as shown by the labour distribution should, of course, balance to or be capable of reconciliation with the payroll for the same period.

A number of cost problems can arise with regard to items such as overtime premiums, shift pay differentials and training costs. Normally such extra or excess labour costs, as they are sometimes termed, are treated as part of the factory overhead and distributed accordingly. However, if they tend to amount to a significant portion of total labour costs over a substantial part of the year, there is some logic in favour of charging directly the jobs or processes that gave rise to the excess costs if they can be identified. In support of this approach, it can be argued that there is also no reason to penalize total production in the plant for abnormal conditions in one or two departments.

Under a standard cost system, such excess costs will soon be reflected in the labour and overhead variances. At this point, management will have to decide if large variances can be tolerated; or, if it is evident that the increased costs are here to stay, the best approach may be to incorporate them into the standards.

The effect of variations in rates of pay or the productivity of labour in a standard cost system may be illustrated by reference again to THE OLD-LINE MANUFACTURING COMPANY. Earlier it was stated that production for the month in the Moulding Department was 20,300 chairs. If the production standards call for the expenditure of 12 minutes of direct labour per chair, the standard direct labour applied for the month would be 20,300 × 12/60 or 4,060 hours. Assuming also that the standard rate for the grade of labour used in the Moulding Department was $2.75 per hour, the standard direct labour cost of production would be 4,060 hours @ $2.75 = $11,165. However, in the real world, costs seldom equal the budgeted or standard amount so we should not be surprised if the labour distribution summary shows that the actual direct labour in the department for the month was 4,100 hours at an average rate of $2.85 per hour, or $11,685.

In this example, there are two variances to be sorted out, a rate variance and an efficiency variance. The rate variance is calculated by comparing the cost of the actual hours worked at actual rates and at standard rates, i.e.,

Actual direct labour hours
    at actual rates    — 4,100 hours @ $2.85 = $11,685.00

Actual direct labour hours
    at standard rates — 4,100 hours @ $2.75 =  11,275.00

Direct Labour Rate Variance _____  $    410.00

Similarly, the efficiency variance is calculated by comparing the cost of the actual and standard direct labour hours, both being extended at standard rates:

Actual direct labour hours
    at standard rates — 4,100 hours @ $2.75 = $11,275.00

Standard direct labour hours
    at standard rates — 4,060 hours @ $2.75 =  11,165.00

Direct Labour Efficiency Variance _____  $    110.00

As may be seen by inspection, both the above are debit or unfavourable variances. This conforms to the mechanical rule stated in Chapter 3 that a plus or positive result arising from the subtraction of standard from actual indicates an unfavourable variance.

## • OVERHEAD

Of the three major cost elements, overhead has probably been subject to more analysis and probing than the other two elements combined. In fact, some cost accountants seem to be obsessed with the idea that if overhead is cut into small enough pieces, it will disappear, or at least lose some of its unpleasant attributes. However, extending the analysis of overhead into ever finer distributions seldom promotes an understanding of the nature of this cost on the part of management, or aids in its control. A more rewarding approach is to break down the overhead cost structure into its variable and fixed components, recognizing that the behaviour of each component is quite different at various levels of activity. This is the technique employed in developing the overhead variances under a standard cost system or when direct costing is employed (direct costing is considered in some detail in the next Chapter).

What exactly is overhead? Earlier it was stated that "overhead" or "factory overhead" represented the whole group of costs that made up the factory (mill, plant, works, etc.) indirect expenses in a manufacturing business. We have also seen that materials and labour which cannot be charged directly to the product are classified as indirect expenses, and hence, become a part of overhead. To be more specific, we might say that overhead consists of all factory costs other than direct labour and direct materials. In addition to indirect labour and indirect materials, then, this would include such items as:

> — supplies
> — utilities (light, power, water, etc.)
> — heat
> — maintenance and repairs of machinery
>    and premises (buildings)
> — rent
> — municipal taxes
> — insurance
> — depreciation
> — administrative services (timekeeping,
>    industrial engineering, materials control,
>    factory management, and so forth)

We have also seen that factory overhead is charged to production even under a general accounting system. Cost Accounting goes further than this aggregate allocation and attempts to assign a specific share of overhead to each unit of product produced. How is this accomplished? The process may be summarized as shown in Figure 12.

The term *primary accounts* means a classification of expenses based on the nature or object of the expenses as cited in the above list (supplies, utilities, heat, etc.).

The second distribution to departments is based on the premise that each function or service in the factory should be charged with a proper proportion of the services it uses or the expense it causes. In some cases, this may be directly measurable — as, for example, power used which may be measured on the basis of meters in each department, or supplies consumed which can be directly traced to the using department by analyzing the material requisitions from stores. But what of such general outlays as taxes, insurance and depreciation? The latter must be distributed on some kind of formula since there is no obvious basis for a direct charge. In fact, this is what is done. Some of the typical factors used are

     — floor area of the department

     — value of assets in the department

     — undepreciated capital cost of machinery in the department.

**Figure 12.**

**THE FLOW OF OVERHEAD TO THE PRODUCT:**

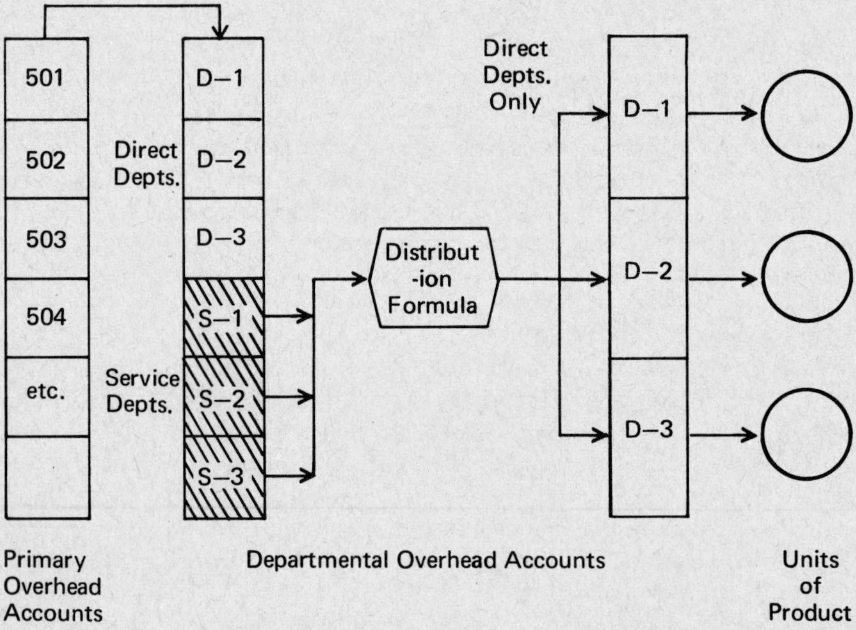

Primary Overhead Accounts     Departmental Overhead Accounts     Units of Product

Having arrived at equitable charges (hopefully) for all overhead expense items in each department, the next step is to develop an equitable formula for charging individual units of product as they are produced.

Some of the more common bases are:
1. Direct Labour Dollars
2. Direct Labour Hours
3. Unit Overhead Method
4. Material Cost
5. Prime Cost
6. Machine Hours

Each one of these is of sufficient importance to be considered separately.

*Direct Labour Dollars*

This method has the advantage of simplicity but it also has some serious limitations, viz.,

(a) It penalizes jobs when high rate operators are assigned to a job for various reasons that should have been assigned to low rated employees.

(b) The contribution of expensive machinery, if any, to the operation is ignored since only the direct labour contribution is costed.

(c) The direct labour dollar is a rather crude measure of the period costs incurred such as taxes, insurance or depreciation, which are a function of time.

In short, unless all labour is paid at approximately the same rates and the skill of the workers does not vary substantially from one operator to another, the direct labour dollar basis cannot be relied upon to produce accurate results. Its only virtue is that it eliminates accounting for hours by jobs or by processes, which would be necessary under the direct labour hours method.

*Direct Labour Hours*

This method overcomes some of the limitations of the direct labour dollar method inasmuch as operations that take the same time to perform are assigned the same amount of overhead regardless of the wages of the operators involved, and it gives recognition to the time factor as a proper basis for measuring most overhead elements. It shares with the direct labour dollar method the limitation that the contribution of machinery is ignored. Hence, if operations are largely automated, it is clearly an inappropriate method for applying overhead.

*Unit Overhead Method*

This method is only applicable where a standard product is produced and there are no important differences in grade or quality among the various sizes or weights of the product produced. In order to arrive at a common unit for dividing into the overhead for the period, weighting factors are usually assigned to each size of the product produced so that a common denominator may be developed.

### Material Cost

The circumstances under which this method would be appropriate are few and far between. It requires a product where the materials are the predominant cost element, where the quantity and cost of material in each product is fairly uniform, and where all products pass through virtually the same process. As in the case of direct labour dollars, it ignores the fact that there may be no correlation between overhead and the cost of materials used, nor is any recognition given to the time factor in processing or the contribution of sophisticated machinery and equipment. In short, it requires an environment where the overhead cost elements are of such slight importance that it makes very little difference to the final total unit cost what basis is used to apply these factors.

### Prime Cost

Prime cost, or the sum of the direct material and direct labour cost elements in the product, suffers from the same lack of objectivity as the labour dollar and material cost methods. Its main virtue is simplicity of calculation, and the only circumstances where it could be safely applied is one in which overhead is a relatively insignificant proportion of total cost. Otherwise, it simply combines all the disadvantages of the direct labour dollars and material cost methods.

### Machine Hours

Where machinery and equipment constitute the major factor in the productive process, the machine hour rate is the most objective method for applying overhead. It requires, of course, the accumulation of machine times for each operation which may add to the expense of cost-finding. However, if accuracy is desired in overhead costing, there is no more theoretically sound method when a high degree of automation applies in the factory.

•    •    •

None of the above methods is mutually exclusive in the sense that a plant-wide approach is required. Thus, in departments where the operations are largely manual, the direct labour hours method would be appropriate; in others where production is largely a function of machine speeds, the machine hours method would obviously be most suitable. Hence, a fine sense of discrimination is required in determining the overhead allocation basis in any given situation, involving consideration of not only what will produce the most accurate results, but also the price to be paid for a high degree of accuracy in terms of the clerical labour and expense in arriving at such optimum costs.

## Figure 13.

### MOULDING DEPARTMENT
### MONTHLY OVERHEAD EXPENSE BUDGET
(at various operating levels)

| | | | | |
|---|---|---|---|---|
| Direct Hours | 3,700 | 3,900 | 4,100 | 4,300 |
| Percent Capacity | 95% | 100% | 105% | 110% |
| *Variable Costs:* | | | | |
| Indirect labour | $ 641 | $ 675 | $ 709 | $ 743 |
| Indirect materials | 320 | 337 | 355 | 371 |
| Shop supplies | 57 | 60 | 63 | 66 |
| Fuel | 237 | 250 | 262 | 275 |
| Utilities | 95 | 100 | 105 | 110 |
| Maintenance, machinery | 428 | 450 | 474 | 495 |
| | $1,778 | $1,872 | $1,968 | $2,060 |
| *Fixed Costs:* | | | | |
| Supervision | $ 525 | $ 525 | $ 525 | $ 525 |
| Administrative services | 650 | 650 | 650 | 650 |
| Rent | 600 | 600 | 600 | 600 |
| Municipal taxes | 550 | 550 | 550 | 550 |
| Insurance | 63 | 63 | 63 | 63 |
| Depreciation | 420 | 420 | 420 | 420 |
| | $2,808 | $2,808 | $2,808 | $2,808 |
| *Total, All Charges* | $4,536 | $4,680 | $4,776 | $4,868 |
| Normal Overhead Rate per hour: | | | | |
| Variable | | 0.48 | | |
| Fixed | | 0.72 | | |
| Total | | 1.20 | | |

Under a standard cost system, the calculation of the overhead variances involves a comparison of four separate factors:

1. The actual overhead expenses for the period. The latter is simply the sum of the balances in the departmental overhead accounts.
2. The allowed budget for actual hours worked. The source of this data is a flexible budget for the department, a schedule similar to Figure 13 above.

3. Actual hours worked costed at the standard or normal overhead rate.

4. The standard overhead in the production for the period. This is derived by multiplying the number of units produced by the standard hour content (direct labour hours or machine hours) as shown by the standard cost cards or specification sheets for the products in question. These standard hours are then extended at the normal overhead rate. The latter is usually calculated by dividing the budgeted expenses at the 100% capacity level by the forecast hours at this same level. Note that 100% capacity seldom means the practical productive capacity of the plant; most often it is the capacity required to satisfy the sales forecast over a period of a year or other time span that is considered appropriate when the overhead budgets are developed.

Returning once more to our example of THE OLD-LINE MANUFAC-TURING COMPANY, it may be recalled that the production for the month in the Moulding Department was 20,300 chair seats and backs which had a standard direct labour hours content of 4,060 hours. Thus, if the standard normal overhead rate is $1.20 per hour, the standard overhead in the production for the month is 4,060 × $1.20 = $4,872.

Actual hours worked, however, totalled 4,100 which represents 105% of capacity as shown by the flexible budget schedule.

In summary, then, the factors required to determine the three orthodox overhead variances are:

1.1 Actual overhead for the period .................................... $4,834

2.1 Allowed budget for the actual hours worked
(4,100 hours) as per the flexible budget schedule .... 4,776

3.1 Actual hours at the standard rate
(4,100 @ $1.20) ........................................................ 4,920

4.1 Standard hours at the standard rate
(4,060 @ $1.20) ........................................................ 4,872

Based on these factors and the formulae cited above in Chapter 3, the variances may now be calculated as follows:

Overhead Spending Variance — Difference between (1) actual overhead expense for the period and (2) allowed budget for the actual hours worked, or $4,834 — $4,776 = $58 DR.

Overhead Efficiency Variance — Difference between (1) actual hours at standard rates and (2) standard hours in the product at standard rates, or $4,920 — $4,872 = $48 DR.

Overhead Volume Variance — Difference between (1) allowed budget for the actual hours worked and (2) actual hours at standard rates, or $4,776 — $4,920 = $144 CR.

PROOF: Actual overhead expenses ................................ $4,834

      Standard overhead applied to work-in-process
      (standard hours × standard rate) .................... $4,872

      Net difference ............................................... ($38)

. . . which is the sum of the three variances sorted out above.

It will be seen that two of these variances are debit or unfavourable variances, while one is a credit or favourable variance — but what is their significance?

The first, or spending variance, simply means that the department incurred $58 more cost than the budgeted allowance for the attained level of activity (4,100 hours). What particular expenses were responsible for this variance can be readily pinpointed through an item-by-item comparison of the schedule of actual overhead expenses for the month with the flexible budget.

The efficiency variance reflects the cost (at the normal or standard overhead rate of $1.20 per hour) of taking 40 more hours to produce the output for the period than the standards allow.

The volume variance is a measure of the implied overabsorption of fixed costs as a result of operating at 200 hours above the normal level, or the level at which the normal overhead rate was set. Thus at 100% capacity, the normal overhead rate is $4,680/3,900 hours = $1.20 per hour. At this same level, the fixed cost portion of this rate is $2,808/3,900 hours = $0.72 per hour. If the level of activity in the department exceeds the normal level of 3,900 hours, then, fixed expenses will be overabsorbed at the standard rate of $0.72 per hour — in this case, 200 hours @ $0.72 = $144.

This is not an easy idea to grasp for individuals who have not been trained in the discipline of Cost Accounting. In fact, such concepts as under- or overabsorbed overhead, loss on idle capacity, profit from intensive use of facilities, and so forth, have long been a stumbling block to a clear understanding of conventional or absorption cost accounting on the part of nonfinance-oriented executives. This, in part, explains the growing popularity of Direct Costing, a technique that circumvents the problem rather neatly.

● **REFERENCES**

1. *Cost Accountants' Handbook,* edited by Theodore Lang, M.B.A., C.P.A., The Ronald Press Company, New York, 1956, p. 841.

• QUESTIONS AND CASE PROBLEMS

4.01   (a)  What is the function of a stores ledger?

(b)  What business forms are most likely to be used to post receipts and issues in the stores ledger?

4.02   At what point is the decision made that an item of material is to be classified as direct or indirect?

4.03   If material overhead is added to the cost of purchased parts, what happens to the offsetting credit?

4.04   Gate valves used by a plumbing and heating contractor cost $8.60 each plus federal sales tax of 12% and provincial sales tax of 5% applied in this order. Material overhead is estimated to amount to 14¢ per valve. Calculate the unit cost (to the nearest cent) at which these valves should be charged to work orders.

4.05   The receipts and issues of a raw material item during the month were:

| Day | 1 on hand | 2,000 @ $0.015 |
|---|---|---|
| | 2 issued | 600 |
| | 5 issued | 1,200 |
| | 10 received | 3,000 @ $0.0166 |
| | 12 issued | 1,000 |
| | 15 issued | 700 |
| | 19 issued | 500 |
| | 24 received | 3,000 @ $0.0175 |
| | 29 issued | 500 |
| | 30 issued | 1,000 |

Calculate the total and per-unit dollar value of the month-end balance for this item using each of the following methods for valuing issues:

(a)  FIFO

(b)  LIFO

(c)  Average Cost

4.06   For the week ended last Saturday, the *attendance card* of Victor Versatile showed the following hours:

MON.  8
TUES. 8½
WED.  9½
THUR. 8
FRI.   8

For the same period, he submitted 13 daily *labour tickets* showing the following charges:

| TICKET NUMBER | DESCRIPTION OF WORK | TIME IN HOURS |
|---|---|---|
| 17773 | Job #328 | 2¾ |
| 17791 | Clean-up | ½ |
| 18003 | Overhaul lathe T006 | 4½ |
| 18024 | Job #336 | 5 |
| 18038 | Clean-up | ¼ |
| 18042 | Job #337 | 3 |
| 18066 | Job #337 | 5½ |
| 18070 | Set up milling machine M63 | 2 |
| 18082 | Job #340 | 2 |
| 18095 | Job #340 | 8 |
| 19003 | Crating shear blades | 2 |
| 19021 | Clean-up | ¼ |
| 19035 | Job #342 | 5½ |

Jobs in the "300" series represent direct labour. Indirect labour accounts are provided in the overhead cost structure as follows:

number 504 Sweeping and cleaning
508 Set-ups
510 Machinery repairs
513 Boxing and loading
515 Overtime premiums
519 Unapplied time

The base rate for this employee is $2.40 an hour. Any hours in excess of 8 on a given day are considered to be overtime, and are paid for at time-and-a-half.

Calculate Victor Versatile's total payroll earnings for the week and the dollar distribution of his time.

4.07 Name six common bases for applying overhead to individual units or batches of product produced. Must the same basis be used in all departments of a plant or factory?

4.08 (a) What is the advantage of using a normal as compared to an actual overhead rate? Illustrate your answer by computing actual rates for each month of the year from the following data, and a recommended normal rate to be used in every month of the year.

| MONTH | FACTORY OVERHEAD | DIRECT LABOUR HOURS |
|-------|-----------------|---------------------|
| Jan. | $48,000 | 12,000 |
| Feb. | 48,000 | 10,000 |
| Mar. | 48,000 | 6,000 |
| Apr. | 48,000 | 4,000 |
| May | 48,000 | 8,000 |
| June | 48,000 | 7,500 |
| July | 48,000 | 6,000 |
| Aug. | 48,000 | 5,000 |
| Sept. | 48,000 | 7,500 |
| Oct. | 48,000 | 8,000 |
| Nov. | 48,000 | 10,000 |
| Dec. | 48,000 | 12,000 |

(b) If the normal rate developed in (a) above is used consistently for the first six months of the year, what will be the amount of over- or underabsorbed overhead at June 30th? Would you recommend revising the rate at this date?

4.09 FULLCOST LIMITED includes an allowance of $2 for selling and administrative expenses in its per-unit overhead standard cost. Since generally accepted accounting principles require that nonfactory costs be excluded from the balance sheet valuation of inventories, calculate the revised valuation of the inventories for financial report purposes and the amount of the adjustment necessary to eliminate this factor from work-in-process and finished goods at December 31st.

The standard unit costs used by FULLCOST LIMITED are:

| | |
|---|---|
| Material | $12.00 |
| Labour | 4.00 |
| Overhead | 5.00 |
| | $21.00 |

Work-in-process at December 31 comprised 6,000 units in the following stages:

| | | |
|---|---|---|
| Material | 70% | complete |
| Labour | 25% | " |
| Overhead | 25% | " |

Finished goods totalled 2,000 units.

4.10 The DISTILLATION DEPARTMENT in an automated chemical plant operates 24 hours a day on each working day of the month. The entire machinery configuration required in the process is controlled by a computer operated by one man on each 8-hour shift.

During the month under review, the DISTILLATION DEPARTMENT operated for 20 days on a continuous 24-hour basis except for 2 hours down time per day during the 3rd shift to enable preventive maintenance to be carried out. During this down time, regulations require the console operator to be present.

Hourly wages paid to the operators were at the following rates:

> 1st shift — 8:00 A.M. to 4:00 P.M. — $3.00
> 2nd shift — 4:00 P.M. to Midnight — $3.42½
> 3rd shift — Midnight to 8:00 A.M. — $3.75

Overhead costs for the month amounted to $7,172.00 and 22,000 gallons of distillate were produced.

The Vice-President, Manufacturing wishes to know the total departmental hourly cost rate. The Cost Accountant feels this would produce inaccurate per-gallon costs since direct labour and overhead are always applied separately in other departments of the company.

Calculate a combined machine hour rate (labour + overhead) for the month and also separate rates for each cost element; then show that the per-gallon unit cost developed by both approaches is identical.

4.11 In the DISTILLATION DEPARTMENT problem (4.10 above), would it have been appropriate to allocate the overhead of the department to each gallon produced using the *direct labour dollars* method? (Give reasons for your answer.)

4.12 THE PORPHYRIC MANUFACTURING COMPANY LIMITED produces concrete pipe for the construction industry. The departmental costs for the month just ended were as follows:

| | BUILDING SERVICE | MATERIALS HANDLING | PIPE FORMING | PIPE CURING |
|---|---|---|---|---|
| Cement | | | $14,800 | |
| Aggregate (sand) | | | 1,220 | |
| Salaries and wages | $720 | $600 | 1,726 | $578 |
| Direction departmental expenses | 790 | 280 | 1,936 | 678 |
| Area of production departments (square feet) | | | 9,060′ | 6,040′ |

Production statistics for the period were:

PIPE FORMING:
| | |
|---|---|
| work-in process, beginning: $3,312 | 800 tons, 90% complete |
| units started | 5,400 tons |
| loss through breakage | 300 tons |
| work-in-process, ending | 1,000 tons, 52% complete |

PIPE CURING:
| | |
|---|---|
| work-in-process, beginning | nil |
| work-in-process, ending | 1,000 tons, 60% complete |

The costs of the Building Service Department are allocated to the Producing Departments on the basis of area, and the costs of the Materials Handling Department on the basis of finished units of production transferred to the next department or to the finished pipe stockpile.

Calculate the unit costs per ton of pipe in each producing department using the "unit costs of the period" method, and assuming the cost of pipe lost through breakage is borne by the remaining units.

4.13  (a) How does a "distribution formula," such as illustrated in Figure 12, enter into the determination of overhead costs?

(b) Were any distribution formulae used by THE PORPHYRIC MANUFACTURING COMPANY LIMITED in 4.12 above? If so, describe.

4.14  THE MADOC MANUFACTURING COMPANY uses a standard cost system, and its standards per unit are:

| | | |
|---|---|---|
| Direct material | — 8 lbs. @ $1.00 per lb. | $ 8.00 |
| Direct labour | — 4 hrs. @ $2.00 per hr. | 8.00 |
| Factory overhead — | $1.20 per | |
| | direct labour hr. | 4.80 |
| | | $20.80 |

For the period ended last month, the records of the Company reflect the following transactions:

(1) Materials purchased, 31,000 lbs. @ $1.04 per lb.

(2) Materials used, per requisitions, 24,500 lbs.

(3) Actual direct wages, 12,500 hours at an average rate of $1.98 an hour.

(4) Actual overhead expenses, $15,300. The allowed overhead for the attained level of activity (12,500 hours) was $14,960 as shown by the Company's flexible budget tables.

(5) Production for the month was 3,100 units, and there was no work-in-process at the beginning or end of the month.

Calculate the seven common variances that would be developed by the standard cost system and indicate in each case whether favourable (credit) or unfavourable (debit).

4.15  Assuming that the overhead is applied to production at standard, as is usually the case in an orthodox standard cost system, what is the amount of over- or underabsorbed overhead that THE MADOC MANUFACTURING COMPANY experienced in the period under review? (Refer to the data in 4.14 above.) Do all the overhead variances developed by the standard cost system account for this over- or underabsorbed balance?

4.16 The overhead volume variance measures the implied under- or over-absorption of fixed costs arising from working more or less than the "normal" number of hours, the level at which the overhead rate was set. Assuming that 12,300 direct labour hours per month is the "normal" level for THE MADOC MANUFACTURING COMPANY,

(a) from the data in 4.15 above, calculate the fixed portion of the overhead rate of $1.20 per direct labour hour;

(b) how many units of finished product should be produced at the "normal" level, and what is the standard overhead content in this number of units?

# FIVE

## DIRECT COSTING

---

The term *direct costing* leads us into one of those semantic thickets in which Accounting in general and Cost Accounting in particular seem to abound. Thus, at this point it is necessary to redefine the meaning of "direct." What the *direct* in *direct costing* means is that only variable production costs are treated as product costs, and fixed factory overhead expenses are banished to the realm of period costs, hitherto only inhabited by selling expense and administrative expense according to the rules of conventional or absorption cost accounting. At the same time, there may be some variable selling and administrative expenses which are properly included in the direct costs before arriving at the direct margin on sales — commonly termed the *profit contribution margin* or, when expressed as a percentage, the *p/v ratio* (profit/volume ratio). Sales commissions provide an illustration of a selling expense that clearly varies directly with sales, and there may well be others such as freight-out and a certain amount of travelling expense, to mention some of the more obvious examples. In the administrative expense cost structure, there may also be a number of items that reflect the cost of variable functions such as billing, credit and collection activities, and communications (telephone, telegraph, telex, etc.). However, caution needs to be exercised in classifying as variable the costs generated by such functions. If the departments or sections are staffed for peak periods (as is often the case) the costs they represent may be slightly variable upwards but seldom if ever downwards. Accordingly, it is usually safer to budget for such functions as fixed costs at a fairly high level than to treat them as purely variable.

These examples illustrate a point that warrants emphasis. In Direct Costing there are no semivariable costs. The approach to semivariable costs is to analyze them into their fixed and variable components using a separate account for each component. Borderline cases are classified as either fixed or variable depending upon their predominant characteristics and, generally speaking, the number of such cases can be reduced to a point where the reliability of the direct costing system is not impaired.

One of the most important attributes of Direct Costing is that it focusses attention on the profit/volume relationship in a business. Hence, an understanding of this relationship (or "break-even analysis" to mention another term for the same concept) is perhaps the best introduction to Direct Costing as a whole.

By definition, the break-even point for a business is where:

Sales = Variable Expenses + Fixed Expenses

This break-even equation is more often expressed in the form:

$$S = \frac{F}{r}$$

where    S = Sales at the break-even point;

F = Fixed Expenses; and

r = the p/v ratio mentioned above, or the margin of Sales over Variable Costs expressed as a percentage.

In order to illustrate the use of these formulae, let us assume that the management of THE OLD-LINE MANUFACTURING COMPANY is sufficiently progressive to be interested in the technique of break-even analysis. The first step, then, is to analyze the costs of the business into their variable and fixed components, as illustrated in Figure 14.

For the sake of simplicity, the selling and administrative expenses are assumed to be entirely fixed in their make-up.

Substituting the p/v ratio (r) and the fixed expenses (F) developed by this analysis in the preceding formulae, the break-even sales for the company are calculated to be $2,540,000.

$$\text{or} \quad S = \frac{F}{r}$$

$$= \frac{\$1,219,200}{.48}$$

$$= \$2,540,000$$

PROOF:    At this level, variable costs at 52% of
sales are $2,540,000 × 0.52    = $1,320,800

Fixed costs, as per the
profit/volume analysis schedule    =  1,219,200

TOTAL COSTS    = $2,540,000

These relationships are more often shown graphically than in tabular form on what is known as a "Break-Even Chart," as illustrated in Figure 15.

## Figure 14.

### THE OLD LINE MANUFACTURING COMPANY
### PROFIT/VOLUME ANALYSIS

Year ended December 31, 19—

|  | DOLLARS | % OF SALES |
|---|---|---|
| Net Sales | $3,240,000 | 100.00 |
| **Variable Costs:** | | |
| Direct materials | 849,500 | 26.22 |
| Direct labour | 734,000 | 22.66 |
| Variable Factory Overhead: | | |
| Indirect labour | 90,500 | 2.79 |
| Light, heat, power & water | 10,800 | 0.33 |
| | $1,684,800 | 52.00 |
| Profit Contribution Margin | $1,555,200 | 48.00 |
| **Fixed Costs:** | | |
| Fixed Factory Overhead: | | |
| Supervision | $   50,000 | |
| Indirect labour | 89,500 | |
| Factory supplies | 10,600 | |
| Light, heat, power & water | 35,600 | |
| Miscellaneous factory expense | 28,000 | |
| | $  213,700 | |
| Selling Expenses | 644,600 | |
| Administrative Expenses | 360,900 | |
| | $1,219,200 | |
| Pre-Tax Profit | $  336,000 | |

Figure 15. illustrates in a rather dramatic fashion the aggregate sales volume that must be attained under current cost conditions before a profit is earned or a loss is avoided. After the break-even point has been reached, however, the fixed costs for the year have all been covered and each dollar of sales contributes 48¢ (the current p/v ratio) towards net profit, ignoring for the moment the share taken by various levels of government in the form of income taxes. The p/v ratio, then, is a measure of the number of cents each dollar of sales contributes towards the fixed costs of a business, and ultimately, the net profit.

Another point of interest is the fact that current sales are 22% (approximately) above the break-even volume and hence provide a safety margin of $700,000. ($3,240,000 — $2,540,000). Stated another way, sales could fall by $700,000 under current cost conditions before the Company would experience a loss.

A number of assumptions about the behaviour of income, cost and

### Figure 15.

## THE OLD LINE MANUFACTURING COMPANY
## BREAK-EVEN CHART

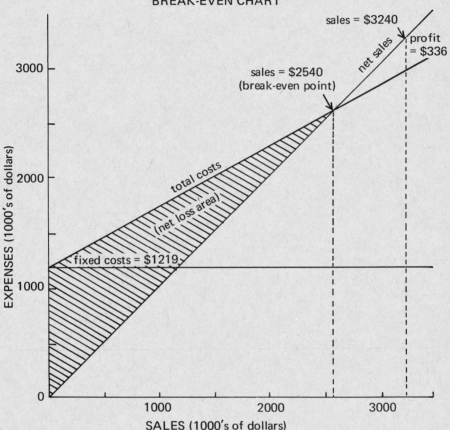

volume underlie the construction of a break-even chart, and changes in this expected behaviour will, of course, cause a shift in the break-even point. That is, the break-even chart may depict relationships that are quite valid but only within a reasonable range of activity, termed the "relevant range" by Horngren[1] who points out that it would be more realistic if the lines were not extended back to the origin but were drawn as illustrated on the next page.

At this point, it should be evident that "break-even analysis," "profit/ volume analysis" and "Direct Costing" are merely alternate terms for the same approach to cost determination. The major advantage of Direct Costing over conventional or absorption costing is that it avoids distortion of operating results when production volume fluctuates to a considerable

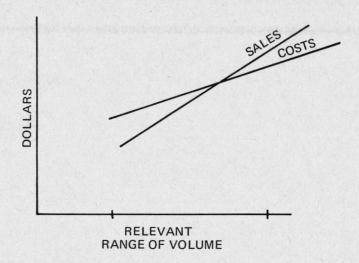

extent from one period to another. Explanations of volume variances to non-accounting executives are seldom understood; the terms "under-" and "overabsorbed overhead" simply do not make sense to them. On the other hand, the results shown by Direct Costing are generally logical and require no such explanation.

There are, of course, circumstances in which Direct Costing is obviously inappropriate. In the mining or extractive industries and in shipbuilding, for example, where the production cycle may extend well beyond a year, charging off all the fixed overheads on an annual basis will not result in a proper matching of costs with the income of the business. It should be noted, however, that both Direct Costing and conventional or absorption cost accounting must produce substantially the same results over a period of years, since sales cannot continuously exceed production, nor can production continuously exceed sales. [2]

In addition to permitting calculation of the break-even point, the safety margin of sales, and so forth, the use of Direct Costing in management reports often greatly facilitates the comparison of actual operating results with a budget or predetermined profit plan. To illustrate, let us assume that the budget for the same year covered by the profit/volume analysis schedule was as follows:

| | |
|---|---|
| Net Sales | $3,000,000 |
| Variable Costs | 1,530,000 |
| Profit Contribution | $1,470,000 |
| % of Sales (p/v ratio) | (49%) |
| Fixed Costs | 1,200,000 |
| Budgeted Pre-Tax Profit | $ 270,000 |

Based on this forecast or budget and the actual operating results set forth in the preceding profit/volume analysis schedule (see Figure 14.), a meaningful report along the following lines may be prepared for management:

For the year ended December 31, 19—, the Company budgeted for a pre-tax profit of $270,000. The actual profit was $336,000 representing an increase of $66,000 over the forecast. The major factors contributing to this favourable variance may be summarized as follows:

SALES exceeded the forecast by $240,000 which, at the normal p/v ratio of 49%, increased profits by ............... $117,600

PROFIT CONTRIBUTION MARGIN was 1% below normal (as a result of an unforeseen increase in certain variable costs) which, on an actual sales volume of $3,240,000, caused a decrease in profits of ................................ (32,400)

FIXED COSTS exceeded the budget by .......................... (19,200)

Resulting INCREASE in PRE-TAX PROFIT
($336,000 — $270,000) .................................... $ 66,000

An item-by-item comparison of the individual items that make up the aggregate variable and fixed costs — *actual,* and the *budget* projected on the basis of actual sales — will disclose in as much detail as may be required what items were ultimately responsible for the summary variances mentioned in the report. It should be noted also that two important factors other than a simple increase in variable costs could cause a variance in the p/v ratio — a sales price variance and a sales mix variance. That is, selling prices on some or all products may have varied from those contemplated by the budget, and the proportions of the various products sold may also have differed from the original forecast. However, such variances can be readily sorted out by analysis and appropriate comments thereon included in the financial officer's report to management. It is possible, of course, to build a similar report around the conventional variances developed by a standard cost system (such as illustrated in Figure 10) but, as mentioned earlier, management generally finds overhead volume variances rather hard to digest.

Direct Costing is also most useful in determining the profit contribution of a division, a department, or a product line. In fact, it is perhaps in the sphere of marketing that the greatest potential of Direct Costing is realized. That is, contribution margins are a necessary factor in arriving at sound answers to such questions as:

— If we decide to reduce our average price by 10%, how much additional volume will be required to produce the same dollar profit?

— If we increase our advertising budget, what additional volume is required to cover the additional outlay involved in this promotional effort?

— What products should be pushed in order to maximize profits, and are there any products in our line which should be dropped?

These and other critical questions can be readily answered by the technique of Direct Costing and graphically presented, if desired, by means of a break-even chart. The point to be recognized is that, other things being equal, the higher the p/v ratio the more rapidly a given volume of sales will cover fixed expenses and produce a net profit. Conventional accounting with its emphasis on "gross profit" tends to obscure this fact. Thus, it is possible to come to erroneous decisions when developing sales or marketing policies on the basis of the "whole cost" of a product. This is perhaps best illustrated by a simple example.

Assume two products with the following selling price and unit cost characteristics:

|  | PRODUCT X | PRODUCT Y |
|---|---|---|
| Selling Price | $9.00 | $9.00 |
| Cost: Variable | 5.85 | 4.95 |
| Fixed | .90 | 2.70 |
|  | $6.75 | $7.65 |
| Gross Profit | $2.25 | $1.35 |
| % of Sales | 25% | 15% |

On the basis of conventional or absorption (whole cost) cost accounting, the natural tendency will be to push Product X because it provides the higher gross profit. A comparison of the contribution margin of each product shows the fallacy of this approach. The product with the higher p/v ratio (in this case, Y) will produce more net income. Ignoring fixed costs for the moment, it is obvious that Product Y has the higher p/v ratio:

|  | PRODUCT X | PRODUCT Y |
|---|---|---|
| Selling Price | $9.00 | $9.00 |
| Variable Cost | 5.85 | 4.95 |
| Contribution Margin | $3.15 | $4.05 |
| % of Sales (p/v ratio) | 35% | 45% |

To demonstrate that pushing Product Y would result in higher profits, compare the actions on the next page.

In some cases, production facilities may limit the practical amounts of a given product which can be made available for sale. Thus, although Product Y is obviously more profitable than Product X, it may take three hours to produce one unit of Y and only one-and-a-half hours to produce a unit of X. Under these circumstances, then, the choice would shift back to X because it produces more profit per hour — i.e.,

|  | X | Y |
|---|---|---|
| Contribution Margin per hour | $2.10 | $1.35 |

| | PUSHING PRODUCT X | PUSHING PRODUCT Y |
|---|---|---|
| Sales (thousands of units) | | |
| X | 90 | 10 |
| Y | 10 | 90 |
| | 100 | 100 |
| Sales in Dollars: | | |
| X @ $9.00 each | $810,000 | $ 90,000 |
| Y @ $9.00 each | 90,000 | 810,000 |
| | $900,000 | $900,000 |
| Variable Costs: | | |
| X @ $5.85 each | $526,500 | $ 58,500 |
| Y @ $4.95 each | 49,500 | 445,500 |
| | $576,000 | $504,000 |
| Contribution Margin | $324,000 | $396,000 |
| Fixed Costs | 180,000 | 180,000 |
| Operating Profit | $144,000 | $216,000 |

In other cases, there may be a wide range in the selling prices for products with the same or near contribution margins. In this situation, emphasis should be placed on those products which will provide the maximum dollar profit contribution most rapidly.

The usefulness of Direct Costing as an aid to decision-making appears in most cases to outweigh its advantages. Possibly the fact that its merits have not achieved widespread recognition among the accounting profession is attributable to the status of Direct Costing in many jurisdictions as an unacceptable basis of inventory valuation for income tax purposes. However, this should not preclude its use throughout the year for internal reporting. When it is desirable to reconcile the operating results on a full cost basis with those produced by Direct Costing, an inventory adjustment can be easily incorporated into the Income Statement or Statement of Profit & Loss and, being shown as a separate item, its effect on reported profits will be clearly seen.

There are other limitations to Direct Costing but as long as they are recognized they do not provide a serious deterrent to its effective use. For example, the fear is often expressed that if a salesman is told what the direct cost of given product is he may tend to feel that any price over this variable cost is satisfactory. However, a commission plan based on contribution margin rather than selling price will effectively discourage this kind of thinking.

With regard to the problem of long-range price determination, it is obvious that a profit-making business must cover full costs in the long run or it will reach a state of insolvency. This simply emphasizes the fact that short-run decisions require information supplied by Direct Costing, while long-run decisions are generally made on the basis of full costs.

- **REFERENCES**

1. *Cost Accounting: A Managerial Emphasis* by Charles T. Horngren, Ph.D., C.P.A., Prentice-Hall Inc., 1962, Englewood Cliffs, N.J., p. 49.

2. *Ibid,* p. 344.

- **QUESTIONS AND CASE PROBLEMS**

5.01   What is the chief attraction that Direct Costing has over conventional or absorption cost accounting from a management standpoint?

5.02   How are costs that are neither entirely fixed nor entirely variable handled under a system of Direct Costing?

5.03   The "break-even equation" is: SALES = VARIABLE COSTS + FIXED COSTS. Express this equation in its more usual form and solve using actual figures based on your own company's operations. If this data is not available, use a hypothetical company with fixed costs of $500,000 and a variable cost ratio of 60%.

5.04   What does the phrase, "safety margin of sales" mean?

5.05   Assuming that an enterprise keeps its accounts on a direct cost basis, specify and explain the meaning of five variances that could account for deviations between the profit plan or budget for a period and the actual operating results.

5.06   Product A has a contribution margin of 20% while product B has a contribution margin of 40%. A sells for $5.00 a unit while B is priced at $7.50 per unit.

   (a)   How many units of each product by itself would have to be sold to produce a profit contribution of $12,000?

   (b)   If the sales forecast calls for sales of A and B in equal proportions, how many units must be sold under these conditions to produce the same profit contribution of $12,000?

5.07   Electricity used by a manufacturing company is charged at the following rates by the Hydro-Electric Power Commission of the municipality in which the company is located:

   1st 1,000 kwh       4.0¢

| Next 2,000 kwh | 2.0¢ |
|---|---|
| Next 4,750 kwh | 1.5¢ |
| etc., | etc. |

These rates apply to the accumulated usage in each rate range, and not simply the consumption between the lower and upper rate levels that define the range.

The company proposes to set up two accounts to distribute the charges from the utility, namely:

Power Cost — Fixed

Power Cost — Variable

Consumption averages 3,600 kwh per month except during July when the plant shuts down for the annual two-week vacation. Consumption in this month drops to approximately 1,500 kwh.

(a) Calculate an annual budget covering the charges that will probably be made to the above two accounts.

(b) How should the Accounting Department distribute the monthly hydro bills from the utility?

5.08 Salesman Black always makes 110% of his quota in terms of gross sales while Salesman White seldom exceeds 80% of his quota. The Sales Manager wants to release White for what he regards as unsatisfactory performance, but the Controller suggests that they analyze the profitability of the sales made by each man. An analysis of the orders booked during a recent week shows that Black often gives a discount of 10% or 20% off list while White always sells at the list price:

| BLACK | | WHITE | |
|---|---|---|---|
| LIST PRICE | ACTUAL SELLING PRICE | LIST PRICE | ACTUAL SELLING PRICE |
| $1,620 | $1,458 | $ 100 | $ 100 |
| 340 | 272 | 325 | 325 |
| 450 | 405 | 1,550 | 1,550 |
| 225 | 180 | 275 | 275 |
| 165 | 165 | 200 | 200 |
| 2,400 | 1,920 | 750 | 750 |

(a) If the contribution margin is 30% of the list price and each man receives a commission of 6% on selling price, which salesman is producing the most profit for the company?

(b) Is your answer any different if the commission is 20% of the contribution margin realized instead of 6% on the selling price?

5.09  The FUNTIME CORPORATION has developed two new types of golfcarts during the current year and reception from the public has been very favourable, possibly because the new lines are priced well below the standard models of golfcarts produced by the Company and its competitors.

The Sales Manager is preparing a forecast for the coming year and has requested some guidance from other department heads as to which of the new lines should be pushed from a sales standpoint. He feels, personally, that one of the new lines should be dropped as both carts are very similar in design and styling and are priced identically. The Cost Department has indicated that, of the two lines, which may be referred to as Type P and Type Q, Type P should be pushed, and they submit the following statistics to support this opinion:

|                      | TYPE P  | TYPE Q  |
|----------------------|---------|---------|
| Selling price        | $15.00  | $15.00  |
| Manufacturing cost   | 10.50   | 12.00   |
| Gross profit         | 4.50    | 3.00    |
|                      | (30%)   | (20%)   |

The Controller, who is familiar with the concepts of Direct Costing, decides that further analysis of the cost of each type is required before a decision can be reached. He ascertains that the manufacturing cost per unit is as follows:

|               | TYPE P  | TYPE Q  |
|---------------|---------|---------|
| Variable cost | $ 6.00  | $ 4.50  |
| Fixed cost    | 4.50    | 7.50    |

The fixed manufacturing costs do not vary regardless of what proportions of P and Q are produced, although the practical capacity of the plant is limited to 110,000 units of both lines. In computing the fixed costs per unit, the Cost Department has assumed that normal production will be 55,000 units of P and 55,000 units of Q annually.

(a) Based on the above information, which one of the new golfcarts should the Company push?

(b) Illustrate the conclusion arrived at in (a) with an operating statement assuming that:

   (1) the Company decides to push type P and sells 100,000 units of P and 10,000 units of Q;

   (2) type Q is stressed, and sales of Q are 100,000 units while sales of P are limited to 10,000 units.

5.10 ARPIC COMPRESSORS LTD. has been operating at a loss since incorporation three years ago. The Directors have agreed to your recommendation that the Company install a system of budgetary control, and you have been appointed Chairman of the Budget Committee to make the necessary plans. A meeting of the Budget Committee is called consisting of the General Manager, the Sales Manager, the Production Superintendent, and yourself, the Comptroller, to prepare some preliminary estimates.

The Production Superintendent states that he does not need a budget; he knows exactly how many compressors the plant can produce and he always plans to produce the maximum (about 3,000 compressors a year), because by doing so, costs are spread over the greatest number of units. As a result, the production cost of each unit is as low as it is possible to make it. He maintains that it is up to the Sales Department to dispose of this output, and they should have no difficulty doing so because manufacturing costs are so low.

The Sales Manager replies that this is nonsense, as the Company has been getting its share of the market for the past three years (about 2,000 compressors annually). In order to sell another 1,000 compressors a year, he estimates that an additional $80 per unit would have to be spent on advertising.

The General Manager suggests that, in any event, they had better stop producing compressors for a while, as the warehousing costs on unsold units are becoming excessive.

The compressors sell for $2,400 each. Material and labour in the production of each unit amounts to $1,500. The fixed factory overhead is $900,000 and fixed expenses of the Sales and General Administration departments total $150,000 annually. Variable selling and administrative expenses amount to $420 per unit.

(a) What is the break-even point for the Company?

(b) Should the Company make the additional outlay of $80 per unit for advertising, and if so, what effect will this have on the break-even volume?

(c) Who will benefit the most from the budget programme — the General Manager, the Sales Manager, the Production Superintendent or the Comptroller?

5.11 The following data relates to the operations of the MINI-RADIO CORPORATION for the last two years:

| | 19-1 | 19-2 |
|---|---|---|
| Sales        (units) | 50,000 | 75,000 |
| Production  (units) | 100,000 | 25,000 |
| Selling price per unit | $20 | $20 |
| Variable cost per unit | $10 | $10 |
| Fixed manufacturing cost per unit | $ 6 | $ 6 |
| Fixed manufacturing costs | $600,000 | $600,000 |
| Fixed selling and administrative expenses | $ 80,000 | $ 80,000 |

The operating statements prepared by the Accountant in conventional form indicate that the Corporation lost money in 19-2 despite the fact that sales increased by 50%. The President feels that these results do not make sense.

(a) Prepare comparative operating statements for both years in conventional form (assuming fixed manufacturing costs are applied to production at standard only) and on a Direct Cost basis.

(b) Draft some interpretive comments for the President explaining the reason for and the significance of the underabsorbed overhead in 19-2 as shown by the conventional operating statement.

5.12 CANADIAN DC INDUSTRIES LIMITED keeps its accounts on a Direct Cost basis. The forecast for the first six months of 19— was as follows:

| | QUALITY PRODUCTS DEPART- MENT | ECONOMY PRODUCTS DEPART- MENT | TOTAL |
|---|---|---|---|
| SALES: | | | |
| 100,000 units @ $8.00 | $  800,000 | — | $  800,000 |
| 600,000 units @ $2.00 | — | $1,200,000 | 1,200,000 |
| | | | $2,000,000 |
| VARIABLE COSTS | 440,000 (55%) | 960,000 (80%) | 1,400,000 (70%) |
| PROFIT CONTRIBUTION | $  360,000 (45%) | $  240,000 (20%) | $  600,000 (30%) |
| FIXED COSTS | 260,000 | 140,000 | 400,000 |
| OPERATING PROFIT | $  100,000 | $  100,000 | $  200,000 |

Actual operating results for the same period were:

SALES:

| | | | |
|---|---|---|---|
| 100,000 units @ $9.00 ............... | $  900,000 | — | $  900,000 |
| 700,000 units @ $1.80 ............... | — | $1,260,000 | 1,260,000 |
| | | | $2,160,000 |
| VARIABLE COSTS ......................... | 540,000 | 945,000 | 1,485,000 |
| | (60%) | (75%) | (68.75%) |
| PROFIT CONTRIBUTION ............. | $  360,000 | $  315,000 | $  675,000 |
| | (40%) | (25%) | (31.25%) |
| FIXED COSTS ............................. | 250,000 | 175,000 | 425,000 |
| OPERATING PROFIT ..................... | $  110,000 | $  140,000 | $  250,000 |

(a) Analyze the variations between actual and forecast operating results by calculating the relevant variances (see 5.05 above).

(b) Write a brief report for management summarizing the factors that caused actual operating profit to vary from the planned operating profit.

# SIX

## RESPONSIBILITY ACCOUNTING

---

The distinction between Responsibility Accounting and Cost Accounting in general is more a matter of emphasis than a difference in concepts and techniques. Thus, under Responsibility Accounting, any expense item or group of costs is regarded as something capable of being traced to a responsible individual. This gives recognition to the fact that, in all organizations, the revenue and expenses do not just happen but are the result of the efforts of individual people who control or approve expenditures and sales effort. Responsibility Accounting also envisages that each individual having supervisory responsibilities can be provided with reports on a regular basis showing his performance in carrying out the activities or functions for which he is accountable.

This implies some difference in the approach to creating departments or cost centres in view of the necessity under Responsibility Accounting of defining rather precisely the area of responsibility of each supervisor and executive. However, such areas of responsibility may be quite compatible with the departmental structure established for cost-finding purposes. As a basis for illustration, it has been assumed that this is the case in THE OLD-LINE MANUFACTURING COMPANY. This is shown in Figure 16 where the aggregate cost structure (see also Figure 3, Chapter 1) has been redefined to show how it would be analyzed under a system of Responsibility Accounting.

The fact that the fixed factory overhead has been excluded from direct departmental costs illustrates another important feature of Responsibility Accounting: there must be no apportionment or proration of an expense. The philosophy of Responsibility Accounting is to designate one individual as the responsible person for each item of expenditure at the level where the expenditure is given final approval. Obviously, this cannot be done if some of the costs of any responsibility area represent apportioned items. If the only individual who has authority to approve a given outlay is the

## Figure 16.

| THE CONVENTIONAL COST STRUCTURE | THE RESPONSIBILITY ACCOUNTING COST STRUCTURE |

| ADMIN. EXPENSES | $360,900 | VICE-PRES. ADMIN. | |
| SELLING EXPENSES | $644,600 | VICE-PRES. SALES | |
| COST OF GOODS SOLD | $1,898,500 | VICE-PRES. MFG. | MOULDING DEPT. SUPT. $697,700 |
| | | | ASSEMBLY DEPT. SUPT. $987,100 |
| | | | FIXED FACTORY O/H $213,700 |

President, then the expenditure is charged to the President's department.

Initially, it might appear under this approach that a lot of items would be classified as charges to the office of the chief executive. However, if this occurs, it should have the salutary effect of forcing management to define the organization more precisely. In short, Responsibility Accounting is highly intolerant of gray areas in the organization, and implies that there shall be no misunderstanding at any level regarding who is responsible for what.

In the case of THE OLD-LINE MANUFACTURING COMPANY, it is assumed that the Vice-President, Manufacturing, has authority to vary the size of his plant by making new capital expenditures or disposing of

**Figure 17.**

THE FLOW OF
RESPONSIBILITY REPORTS (I)

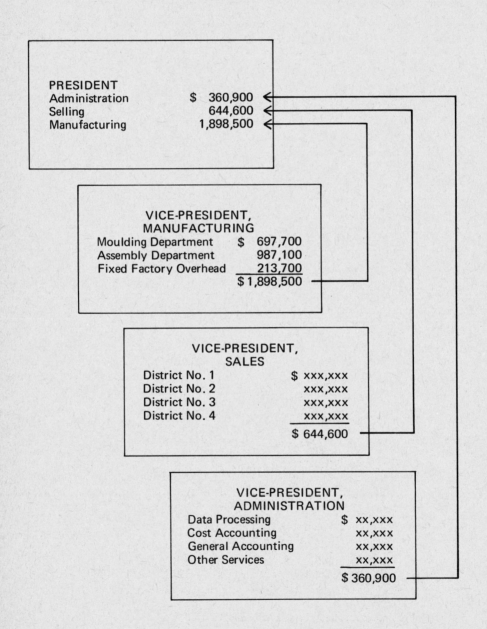

existing facilities, if this action seems appropriate in his considered judgement. Accordingly, he accepts responsibility for the level of fixed costs that the Company's investment in plant and equipment gives rise to — depreciation, taxes, insurance, and so forth — in addition to the controllable items delegated to his subordinates, the Superintendents of the Moulding and Assembly Departments.

This draws attention to another important feature of Responsibility Accounting, the interlocking nature of the responsibility reports produced. Thus, the expenditure (and income, if any) of each level is carried forward to the next level, and so on up to the top of the organization. At the same time, the net result must balance with the summary Statement of Profit & Loss for the company as a whole (see Figure 8, Chapter 2, and Figure 14, Chapter 5). This process is indicated by illustrations in Figures 17 and 18.

**Figure 18.**

### THE FLOW OF
### RESPONSIBILITY REPORTS (II)

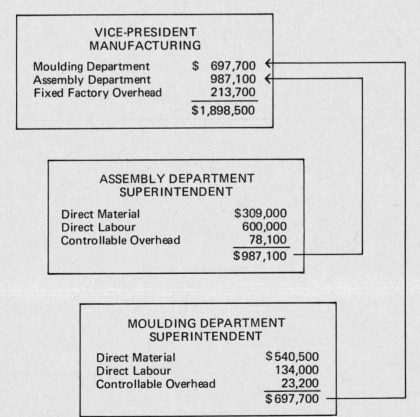

VICE-PRESIDENT
MANUFACTURING

| | |
|---|---:|
| Moulding Department | $   697,700 |
| Assembly Department | 987,100 |
| Fixed Factory Overhead | 213,700 |
| | $1,898,500 |

ASSEMBLY DEPARTMENT
SUPERINTENDENT

| | |
|---|---:|
| Direct Material | $309,000 |
| Direct Labour | 600,000 |
| Controllable Overhead | 78,100 |
| | $987,100 |

MOULDING DEPARTMENT
SUPERINTENDENT

| | |
|---|---:|
| Direct Material | $540,500 |
| Direct Labour | 134,000 |
| Controllable Overhead | 23,200 |
| | $697,700 |

It is generally agreed that there are at least three significant benefits to be derived from a system of Responsibility Accounting. First, the provision of regular reports to supervisors which are custom-designed for their particular functions helps to stimulate an interest in overall corporate goals and tends to make the recipients feel "part of the team," especially if such reports were formerly restricted to the senior management level. A second advantage is that, from a technical standpoint, the elimination of prorations and apportionments of cost may simplify the accounting system and facilitate the data processing runs incidental to the preparation of periodic reports. Third, it is clearly a distinct aid to budgeting. In the final analysis, all budgeting can only be effectively performed by line managers and only with respect to items under their direct control. Hence, the structuring of responsibility and the definition of controllable items, features which are the essence of Responsibility Accounting, provide an optimum starting point or basis for setting budget standards.

Looking at the negative side, it should not be expected that the introduction of a system of Responsibility Accounting will be entirely free from difficulties or obstacles. As every management accountant knows, first line supervisors or foremen are not naturally partial to budgets and accounting reports, regardless of how sound they may be from a management control standpoint. If the responsibility reports involve such people in what they regard as "a lot of unnecessary paperwork," the system will not be an unqualified success. In the installation phase, then, it will be necessary to "sell" Responsibility Accounting to many supervisory personnel, and possibly even a few senior executives. In the process, it is desirable to stress the positive features of Responsibility Accounting, the fact that each responsible individual is being supplied with a tool to exercise real control over his operations — in effect, a custom-tailored accounting system of his own. Hopefully, it will also eliminate most of the "little black books" or private information systems that some managers have felt it necessary to maintain in the past because of the actual or deemed inadequacy of the output from the formal accounting system.

Another deterrent to the adoption of Responsibility Accounting may be the large volume of reports that is generated by the system, taking into account the fact that everyone down to the most junior level of management gets one. This could be a cost consideration in a large organization if they do not have access to high-speed data-processing facilities. On the other hand, it would not be a significant factor in a small business. The secondary benefits, in the form of the organization clarification and general tidying-up of the accounting system that are necessary preliminaries to the introduction of Responsibility Accounting, will usually make the effort well worthwhile for most small and medium size businesses. It should be noted also that, despite the large aggregate total of reports that may be generated, the actual amount of paper which any one individual receives is usually quite small — his own report and copies of those for his immediate subordinates.

Needless to say, When Responsibility Accounting is introduced within a company, all existing control reports that are not integrated into the responsibility reporting system should be discontinued; otherwise, the organization will rapidly find itself drowning in a sea of paper.

● QUESTIONS AND CASE PROBLEMS

6.01 What are the similarities and differences between Responsibility Accounting and Cost Accounting in general?

6.02 What benefits may be expected to accrue from the introduction of a system of Responsibility Accounting?

6.03 Why should it be necessary to "sell" Responsibility Accounting to people?

6.04 Classify the following cost elements as controllable (C) by a departmental foreman or as non-controllable (N). If some part of the cost is controllable and another part is fixed, classify the item as controllable on the assumption that the fixed portion is charged against someone else's budget.

> Building Repairs
> Canada Pension Plan contributions
> Company Pension Plan contributions
> Depreciation
> Idle Time
> Insurance
> Light & Power
> Machinery Repairs
> Municipal Taxes
> Oils & Lubricants
> Overtime Premiums
> Rags & Wipers
> Rent
> Shift Premiums
> Small Tools
> Training

6.05 "Responsibility Accounting won't work in our company. We have to prorate our service department costs across our production departments in order to arrive at true direct department figures for costing each ton of pipe produced."

Discuss this statement by the Production Superintendent of THE PORPHYRIC MANUFACTURING COMPANY LIMITED. Is it true that the nature of the business precludes the use of Responsibility Accounting?

6.06 By the end of the third quarter, the Foreman of the Materials Handling Department had experienced a significant overrun on his costs. Upon analysis, it was discovered that the wage rates of the lift truck operators and other stock handlers had been increased by 15% on July 1, but there had been no change in the rates for charging the direct departments that use the services of the Materials Handling Department.

The Production Manager is reluctant to have the Materials Handling Department increase its charging rates because "this will throw the direct departments several miles off budget too!"

What should be done about the unfavourable variances in the Materials Handling Department?

6.07 The hourly rated employees of THE OLD-LINE MANUFACTURING COMPANY have formed a baseball team, and during the spring season, competitive games are played in an informal league with other plants in the area. The manager of the team has suggested to the Vice-President, Manufacturing that it would be good for employee morale if the Company would provide uniforms for the team and some new equipment (baseball gloves, balls and bats). The estimated cost of this equipment is $750, and the outlay, if made by the Company, would be charged to "Employee Benefits" in the Fixed Factory Overhead cost structure.

The Vice-President, Manufacturing replied that there was no provision for such an expenditure in the budget, but he would discuss the request with the Personnel Manager.

The Personnel Manager, who reports to the Vice-President, Administration, was unable to find any published policy rules covering a request of this nature, and referred the matter to the President.

Are there gaps in the Company's Responsibility Accounting system if this question had to be referred to the President?

6.08    The Advertising Manager in a large company which operates under a system of Responsibility Accounting has complained to his superior, the Vice-President, Marketing, that the reports he gets from the Accounting Department do not agree with the records he keeps of advertising media costs. Upon learning of this complaint from the Vice-President, Finance, the Controller pointed out that the Accounting Department was unable to keep up-to-date with advertising outlays because the Advertising Manager, who is supposed to approve all accounts rendered by the Company's advertising agency, often holds such accounts for four to six weeks before passing them on to the Accounting Department for vouchering and payment.

Does the complaint of the advertising Manager indicate that Responsibility Accounting does not always work?

6.09    MORECHROME MOTORS LIMITED operates a free coffee bar for the convenience of its customers. The costs of this facility, which was initiated by the President, are charged to the New Car Department. The New Car Sales Manager objects to being charged with 100% of the cost of the coffee bar because, as he correctly observes, most of the people who use this facility are service customers waiting to claim their cars while the Service Department Cashier adds up work orders, sends a car jockey to find vehicles, etc.

If a system of Responsibility Accounting is in effect at MORECHROME MOTORS LIMITED, which executive should be charged with the cost of the coffee bar, the New Car Sales Manager or the Service Manager?

6.10    THE INIMITABLE LIFE INSURANCE COMPANY has 105 Branch Offices scattered across the country, each one under the direction of a Branch Office Manager, who in turn reports to one of seven Regional Agency Superintendents. The Head Office management team consists of a Vice-President, Underwriting, a Medical Director, a Claims Superintendent, a Chief Actuary, a Corporate Secretary, a Vice-President, Administration and a Vice-President, Production, the latter being responsible for the activities of the seven Regional Agency Superintendents.

If a system of Responsibility Accounting is introduced involving monthly reports to all managers, how many individual reports will be produced on each report date, assuming all Head Office executives report directly to the President and General Manager, and the Board of Directors (which comprises 11 individuals excluding the President) receives copies of the President's report? (Draft an organization chart to clarify your answer.)

# SEVEN

## SPECIAL PROBLEMS:
## JOINT PRODUCTS AND BY-PRODUCTS

---

The work of a cost accountant would be infinitely simpler if such things as joint products and by-products did not exist. The fact is, however, they do occur with considerable frequency and in some rather important industries. Moreover, the cost determination problems which they present are of considerable interest, not only for themselves, but also because they are analogous to the problems that arise when the techniques of cost accounting are applied to areas outside the factory — for example, the assignment of cost to different kinds of services rendered or to different classes of consumers or customers served.

By definition, *joint products* are two or more products produced by the same processing operations, each having a significant relative sales value. A *by-product* has the same attribute of simultaneity of production (you cannot produce one without getting the other) but its value from a marketing standpoint is not so significant that it would, of itself, be an object of manufacture. Thus, relative sales value is really the key factor in the distinction between a joint product and a by-product. Changes in technology may alter the classification of joint products to that of by-products, and vice versa. The present trend is in the direction of obtaining a 100% yield from all raw material, a process that has resulted in upgrading by-products, in some cases, to the status of joint products. Typifying this trend is the expression current in the meatpacking industry today, "we use everything in a pig except the squeal."

The distinction between the variety of names that are used to describe by-products (or residuals, as they are also frequently termed) may be clarified by picturing a continuum or scale. At the lower end of the scale are to be found *waste products* with no saleable value, while the upper end is occupied by *by-products* with some definite recovery potential as illustrated on the next page.

As a little reflection will show, virtually all industries have these residuals,

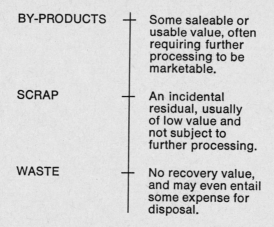

| | |
|---|---|
| BY-PRODUCTS | Some saleable or usable value, often requiring further processing to be marketable. |
| SCRAP | An incidental residual, usually of low value and not subject to further processing. |
| WASTE | No recovery value, and may even entail some expense for disposal. |

and it is simply a question of their economic value whether or not they warrant the designation of by-products.

Joint products may comprise clearly distinct items or varying grades of the same product, as the following representative list of joint product industries indicates:

| INDUSTRY | MAIN OR JOINT PRODUCTS | BY-PRODUCTS |
|---|---|---|
| Flour Milling | — high-grade flour | — low-grade flour<br>— bran<br>— mill feed |
| Lumber (sawmill) | — various grades of lumber | — reconstituted wood (compressed wood scraps)<br>— sawdust |
| Meat Packing | — dressed meats<br>— cured and smoked products<br>— canned meats | — hides<br>— fats (lards & tallows)<br>— pharmaceutical products (glands)<br>— animal feed<br>— fertilizer |
| *Oil Refining | — gasoline | — fuel oil<br>— stove oil<br>— naptha<br>— kerosene<br>— benzine |
| *Steel (coke ovens) | — coke | — sulphate of ammonia<br>— phenol<br>— coal tar<br>— gas |
| Sugar Refining | — various grades of sugar | — molasses<br>— pulp |

*In these industries, the items shown as by-products are sometimes treated as joint products, in which case a proportion of the total process cost prior to the split-off point is allocated to each product.

The two major problems that joint products and by-products present to the cost accountant are:

(1) how to value inventories of joint products and by-products at the end of an accounting period or other date when financial statements are prepared, and

(2) how to apportion the cost of joint products inter se on an objective basis.

## • BY-PRODUCTS

As by-products usually represent a minor facet of a company's overall operations compared to joint products, the problems they raise are not as critical, although this statement is a generalization to which there are inevitable exceptions. As mentioned above, by-products can often change in relative importance as a result of technological advances or new methods of processing that impart an economic value to residuals which they did not possess formerly. Hence, the accounting treatment of by-products should be governed by their significance in the total product line and not by mechanical rules.

As many as seven different methods of by-product accounting have been identified by various writers on the subject although, in reality, two of these are merely variations on the fifth method outlined below. The main features of all by-product costing methods is that no allocation of costs to the by-product takes place prior to the "split-off point" — i.e., the point at which the main product and the by-product can be separately identified. The various methods are as follows:

*1. The "sundry income" method.*

Under this approach, no attempt is made to assign any costs to the by-product and the proceeds from sales of the residual are treated as sundry or non-operating income. This method is only appropriate when the residual in question is close to the "scrap" category on the value scale, and where the sales proceeds are insignificant. If these conditions are not present, the costs of the main or joint products tend to be overstated, and operating results do not reflect a proper matching of costs and revenues.

*2. The "total sales" method.*

Under this method, the proceeds from disposal of the by-product are included in product sales along with the sales of the main product instead of being credited to sundry income. This approach is slightly preferable to the "sundry income" method, although the failure to record the value of period-end by-product inventories may distort the operating results to some extent throughout the year.

*3. By-product sales credited to main product production costs.*

The reasoning behind this method is that the production costs of the main product should be shown at the net amount after deducting any waste or scrap recoveries. As no inventories of by-products are established, it is not much of a refinement over the second method.

*4. "Net yield" from by-product credited to main product production costs.*

The only variation between this approach and method #3 is that a charge for selling and administrative expense is deducted from by-product sales before the resulting "net yield" is applied as a reduction of the costs of the main product.

*5. "Value" of by-product credited to main product production costs.*

Under this procedure, the by-product is charged with any production costs incurred beyond the split-off point as well as an appropriate portion of selling and administrative expense. By-product inventories are also set up, but only based on costs incidental to processing or handling of the by-product subsequent to the split-off point; in some cases, by-product inventories are simply valued at selling price less selling and administrative expense. The net "value" of the by-product — sales less expenses attributable thereto — is then applied as a reduction of the main product's production cost. This approach has the merit that period-end inventories of by-product are established, thereby permitting the credit to the main product to be made in the same period in which the by-product emerges, not when actual sales take place, which may be at irregular intervals.

●    ●    ●

Needless to say, any costs incurred to finish or market the by-product must be justified by making possible a sales return beyond the split-off point that will more than cover such additional expense. Otherwise, it would be more profitable to sell the by-product in an "as is" condition as soon as it materializes, or if this is not possible, simply to dump it. By-product costs and by-product revenues are marginal costs and marginal revenues, and any costs incurred prior to the split-off point are irrelevant in arriving at a decision as to whether or not further processing is warranted.

● JOINT PRODUCTS

As has been inferred up to this point, the distinction between a by-product and a joint product is a matter of relative sales value. If the output from the same productive process is two or more products each one of which represents a significant sales value, they must be regarded as joint products rather than by-products, even though the principal object of manufacture is to produce only one of them — e.g., No. 1 grade tobacco leaf.

Three methods represent the most widely adopted solutions to the problem, although many variations on each can be identified in specific industries. Each method is also subject to a number of objections on theoretical or practical grounds which tend to suggest that this is one of the unsolved problems of cost accounting. This is the view taken by Lanza who makes the statement that "accounting theory for joint and by-products is incomplete." [1]

### 1. The average unit cost method.

The theoretical basis for this method is that the profits of an enterprise arise from the sale of all its products and it is not possible to determine the profit contribution of any single product — at least under conditions of joint cost. Another argument for the method is that, with regard to joint products, one cannot claim that it costs more per unit to produce one than the other when they all represent the output from the same process. Accordingly, for inventory purposes, any unsold product is simply valued at average per unit cost determined by dividing total production costs by the aggregate number of units produced. It should be noted that this approach is only taken in those industries where the joint products represent varying grades of the same product (e.g., lumber). It does not make sense to a meat packer to value filet mignon at the same per pound cost as blade roast, for example, or for an oil refinery to cost gasoline at the same per gallon price as kerosene. This point underlines the apparent weakness of the average unit cost method: no weight is given to the relative market values of the various joint products in apportioning costs at the split-off point — but is this a valid consideration?

### 2. The physical attribute method.

Under this approach, each joint product is costed on the basis of weight, volume, chemical content or other attribute that represents a convenient unit of measurement for the raw material entering into each product. This method suffers from the same limitations as the first method when it is applied to different grades of the same product: the selling prices of the high grade products will tend to show a high profit margin while the low grade products will tend to be loss items. If the products are distinctly separate items, physical factors do not provide an objective basis for comparison. Thus, 100 pounds of coke is not the same thing as 100 pounds of sulphate of ammonia. Their weights may be identical but their substances are quite different.

### 3.  *The market value method.*

Market values provide the basis for allocating joint costs under this method. That is, at the split-off point, the common costs of the process are apportioned to each joint product in proportion to its final selling price. If no further processing is required subsequent to the split-off point, this will have the effect of assigning the same profit margin to each product.

There is a certain logic to the results produced by this method which appeals to the layman. Thus, products with a relatively high selling price bear a proportionately higher share of the common cost — giving support to the common belief that market prices must reflect the cost of an item. It should be noted, however, that the costs of the "high-value" products under this method are being weighted so that the products with a low yield in terms of selling prices will also show a profit on their sale. This may be quite satisfactory to management, or in accordance with what they feel the operating results should show. Nevertheless, it should be recognized that this basis is really no more objective than any of the preceding methods.

•   •   •

If there is any conclusion to be drawn from an examination of joint product costing techniques it is that such costs are not useful for profit planning but only for inventory valuation purposes. By profit planning is meant the determination of the best product mix or the optimum output that will maximize profit. If there is some discretion possible in the quantities in which a package of joint products can be produced, opportunities for this sort of planning exist. In these circumstances, the aggregate revenue from the entire package of joint products must be balanced against the cost of producing the package.

To illustrate, let us assume that a joint product package is always produced in the following proportions:

| Grade | — | A | 40% |
|-------|---|---|-----|
|       | — | B | 20% |
|       | — | C | 15% |
|       | — | D | 15% |
|       | — | E | 10% |

. . . and that market prices for A tend to decline sharply as the supply is increased but that prices for the remaining products do not fluctuate to any significant degree. Hence, at various outputs from 10,000 to 40,000 aggregate units the net yield from the package is as follows:

(1)   10,000 units:

| | | | |
|---|---|---|---:|
| 4,000 A @ | $2.20 | — | $ 8,800 |
| 2,000 B @ | .80 | — | 1,600 |
| 1,500 C @ | .50 | — | 750 |
| 1,500 D @ | .40 | — | 600 |
| 1,000 E @ | .25 | — | 250 |
| | | | $12,000 |

(2)   20,000 units:

| | | | |
|---|---|---|---:|
| 8,000 A @ | $1.60 | — | $12,800 |
| 4,000 B @ | .80 | — | 3,200 |
| 3,000 C @ | .50 | — | 1,500 |
| 3,000 D @ | .40 | — | 1,200 |
| 2,000 E @ | .25 | — | 500 |
| | | | $19,200 |

(3)   30,000 units:

| | | | |
|---|---|---|---:|
| 12,000 A @ | $1.00 | — | $12,000 |
| 6,000 B @ | .80 | — | 4,800 |
| 4,500 C @ | .50 | — | 2,250 |
| 4,500 D @ | .40 | — | 1,800 |
| 3,000 E @ | .25 | — | 750 |
| | | | $21,600 |

(4)   40,000 units:

| | | | |
|---|---|---|---:|
| 16,000 A @ | $0.40 | — | $ 6,400 |
| 8,000 B @ | .80 | — | 6,400 |
| 6,000 C @ | .50 | — | 3,000 |
| 6,000 D @ | .40 | — | 2,400 |
| 4,000 E @ | .20 | — | 800 |
| | | | $19,000 |

In this case, maximum yield is obtained from an output of A somewhere around 12,000 units, a conclusion which would be obscured by looking at the apportioned cost, and hence, the theoretical margin of any individual product in the package. This is one of those situations where it is better not to push the costing analysis down to the elementary level.

Not all organizations are profit-making entities, but management or the trustees, as the case may be, would still like to know the cost of the various joint products or services offered. This applies to a rather important group of organizations such as charitable foundations and welfare agencies who have only in recent years become aware of the techniques of cost accounting.

In applying costing techniques to such organizations, the first step is to analyze the activities into the functions or programs carried on, a process not unlike the departmentalization that is required in an industrial enterprise in order to permit a scientific or reasonably objective distribution of overhead expenses. The fixed costs (other than administrative overhead) are then allocated to the functions identified upon the best basis available—usually area of space occupied by each function or service, if they share a common premises. These fixed costs would include such items as rent, taxes, light, heat and so forth.

The variable costs are a little easier to allocate since the bulk of these is usually represented by salaries of case workers, technicians, psychiatrists and other professionals, whose time can be measured by means of time reports, number of cases handled, and so forth.

Finally, there is a group of fixed costs for which there would appear to be no objective basis for distribution to function. This is the administrative or general overhead of the organization, including such items as the salary of the executive director and the salaries of the clerical staff and administrative assistants who perform services for all functions. Other office costs such as telephone service, accounting and data processing, are part of the same cost structure.

On the assumption that the administration of any organization is basically a function of people, these costs are generally prorated to the various functions in proportion to the number of permanent employees and volunteers attached to each function. If this method proves too complicated to calculate, a simpler approach is to use payroll dollars as the basis—that is, the direct salary distribution before any allocation of indirect salaries contained in the administrative overhead itself.

Regardless of the method employed, it is important that everyone concerned with the financial reports of the organization shall understand the assumptions behind such prorations. Ideally, there should be a clear separation in the financial reports between direct charges to functions and apportioned expenses. Bearing in mind that there is really no objective basis for apportioning fixed overhead, whether a profit-making or nonprofit organization is involved, it is preferable to treat all fixed indirect expenses as a separate pool of costs not subject to proration. The latter approach must be taken, initially in any case, if budgetary control is to be exercised.

● REFERENCE

1. *Accounting for Joint Products and By-Products* by Ralph M. Lanza, Cost and Management, April, 1965, p. 148.

● QUESTIONS AND CASE PROBLEMS

7.01 What attributes do waste, scrap and by-products have that enables a distinction to be made between them?

7.02    When is it preferable to simply discard a by-product instead of attempting to market it?

7.03    When does a by-product become a joint product, and vice versa?

7.04    What problems do joint products and by-products present to a cost accountant?

7.05    What is the meaning of the term "split-off point"?

7.06    Are period-end inventories of by-products usually recorded for financial statement purposes?

7.07    A lumber mill has to pay $4 a ton to have its excess sawdust carted away and disposed of in the local municipal dump (approximately 5 tons monthly). By installing a special purpose machine costing $12,000, the the sawdust can be converted into reconstituted wood panels, 4' x 8' having a thickness of 3/8". The machine will produce 40 of these panels from each ton of sawdust, each panel having a sales value of $2.40.

If the machine has a useful life of five years and the monthly labour and overhead required to operate it amounts to $212 without taking into account depreciation or capital cost allowance, would it be profitable to make this investment?

7.08    (a) Name the three common methods of joint product costing. Which method, if any, provides the best basis for profit planning?

(b) It will be recalled that the maximum yield for the joint product package illustrated in the text was at approximately 30,000 units for a total revenue of $21,600, i.e.,

| | | | | |
|---|---|---|---|---|
| 12,000 | A | @ | $1.00 — | $12,000 |
| 6,000 | B | @ | .80 — | 4,800 |
| 4,500 | C | @ | .50 — | 2,250 |
| 4,500 | D | @ | .40 — | 1,800 |
| 3,000 | E | @ | .25 — | 750 |
| | | | TOTAL — | $21,600 |

At this output, the total cost of the package is $17,400 and the respective weights of the joint products in the package on a per-unit basis are:

A  —  0.45 lbs.

B  —  1.50 lbs.

C  —  2.50 lbs.

D  —  2.50 lbs.

E  —  2.70 lbs.

Illustrate your answer to (a) by calculating a per-unit cost and gross profit (or loss) for each of the five joint products in the package using each of the three common methods of joint product costing in turn.

7.09   A quarry yields two types of marble: Blaircreek Blue and Wilmot White. The labour and expense involved in cutting out a block of either is identical, but the two types are so intermingled in the quarry that, generally speaking, one cubic foot of Wilmot White must be produced for every cubic foot of Blaircreek Blue. However, the sales value of Blaircreek Blue is almost double that of Wilmot White because of the unique colouring of the former, no similar shade being produced by any other quarry in the country.

How would you recommend that the quarry costs be apportioned between Blaircreek Blue and Wilmot White?

7.10   GROUP PHARMACEUTICALS LIMITED produces a tonic medicine known as Vinovim. The production process involves two departments: Blending and Bottling. At the completion of the process in the Blending Department, a by-product, Vimsalt, is produced, representing by weight 20% of the materials put into production. A further 20% is lost through evaporation during the process, and the balance represents mixed Vinovim ready for bottling. The by-product, Vimsalt, is bagged and sold to a fruit and vegetable canning company at $56.80 per 100 lb. bag.

During the month of June, 19—, a vat of Vinovim was produced involving the following outlays for material and labour:

Vinovim ingredients used   —   5,000 lbs. @ 18¢ per lb.

Bottles used   —   2,375 @ $8.00 per hundred.

Labour — Blending Dept.   —   $600

Labour — Bottling Dept.   —   $360

Overhead is charged to the production departments at a standard rate of 80% of the labour dollar. The packaging of Vimsalt is carried out in the Bottling Department, and this operation is estimated to cost 50¢ per bag of Vimsalt, which is credited to the Bottling Department and charged to the by-product.

A gallon of blended Vinovim weighs 8 lbs.

Calculate: (a) the profit per bag of Vimsalt;

(b) the net cost per gallon of Vinovim produced after deducting the recovery from the by-product.

7.11  Why should the pro rata share of fixed indirect expenses be excluded from departmental figures in applying a system of budgetary control?

7.12  The records of the local branch of a national welfare organization contain the following information relative to the year ended on March 31, 19—

| | |
|---|---|
| Rent, light, heat and other fixed costs | $44,000 |
| Administrative and clerical salaries | 25,000 |
| Accounting, data processing, stationery, telephone and other administrative costs | 10,800 |
| Supplies and other direct costs by function | |
| — Family Counselling | 2,760 |
| — Medical and para-medical services | 6,200 |
| — Public education services | 3,080 |
| Professional salaries and fees (social workers, consulting psychologists, physicians, etc.) | 84,000 |

The time spent by the professional staff based on time reports submitted has been analyzed into:

Family Counselling, 3,360 hours; Medical and related services, 5,600 hours; Education services, 2,240 hours.

The premises occupied by the local branch are utilized in the following proportions:

| | |
|---|---|
| Family Counselling | nil |
| Medical and related services | 60% |
| Public Education services | 15% |
| Administration | 25% |

Prepare an operating statement for the year showing the bases used for allocating the indirect costs to each function. After all costs have been allocated to the specific functions carried on, calculate the cost per hour of each function.

# EIGHT

## COSTS OF THE
## DISTRIBUTION FUNCTION

---

As in the case with a number of terms in accounting, there is not unanimous agreement, even among accountants, as to exactly what *distribution costs* comprise, although most businessmen tend to consider that the term is synonymous with *marketing expenses*. In other words, the definition is assumed to cover all costs associated with persuading present and prospective customers to buy, the costs of the physical handling functions such as warehousing and delivery, clerical expense in connection with the paperwork involved, and possibly some follow-up or service costs after the customer has received the goods.

The author of perhaps the most authoritative recent work on the subject, André Parent, prefers a broader definition: "distribution costs include all expenses incurred after the goods have been made available for sale."[1] Generally speaking, this would include all costs that are traditionally displayed below the "gross margin" line in the Income Statement. Such an omnibus definition is satisfactory provided it is recognized that the allocation of general and administrative overhead to specific products or to specific customers can only be done on a more or less arbitrary basis. At the same time, some items that are often included in the administrative expense cost structure can and should be directly related to the distribution function. This refers to such activities as credit authorization, order filling, invoice preparation, invoice typing, and maintenance of the accounts receivable records. After these costs have been sorted out, however, a residual pool of general management overhead inevitably remains. The customary treatment of such unassigned costs is to allocate them to customers and/or products on a formula basis—as a percentage of sales, for example.

In considering the utility vs. the expense of applying costing techniques to the distribution function, the first question management is likely to ask is, "why analyze distribution costs?" The answer is that, in any given company,

97

there is often a vast potential for profit improvement in the form of reduced marketing costs or more effective marketing practices. Distribution Costing is the alchemy that can convert this potential into a reality.

In the past, manufacturing costs were analyzed and controlled to the *nth* degree while distribution costs were regarded with a surprising amount of fatalism. That is, they were treated as highly inevitable, and very little thought was given towards selective concentration of marketing activities where they would produce the best pay-back. At the other extreme, there has been a tendency at times to overapply the techniques of cost accounting to certain functional areas of distribution with the result that some impressive if rather useless unit costs were developed. Thus, if your accountant tells you that it costs $2.92 to process every order and issue the invoice and $3.52 to collect the account receivable, the initial reaction is likely to be "so what?" and rightly so. Analysis will usually reveal that such unit costs are made up of a fairly high proportion of joint and common costs, so that their application to a given product, a given customer, or a specific territory may have the result of concealing rather than revealing the important characteristics of the activity under study. In other words, the caveat stated by Horngren needs to be kept in view, namely, "cost analysis in marketing is sometimes too much concerned with dividing total costs by units to get a magic unit cost for the wrong purpose."[2] However, if the ultimate goal of the cost analysis being performed is kept in sight at all times—say, to disclose unprofitable lines and unprofitable accounts, to select the most profitable channels of distribution, and so forth—hopefully, this pitfall can be avoided.

The first step in the analysis of distribution costs is to classify the cost elements involved by function. In this connection, it will usually be found that the selling and administrative cost structures do not provide more than half of the breakdowns required. However, it is generally not too difficult to analyze the payroll, for example, in order to find what the personnel costs are within each function. Space costs may not be so easily ascertained (they are frequently common to more than one function), but the problem is no more difficult than that of distributing factory overhead to the departments which give rise to or use a particular cost element or service.

The main activities involved in the distribution function may be classified as:

1. Order-getting.
2. Order-filling.
3. Shipping and delivery.

4.  Credit and collection.

5.  Sales management.

Within these main categories, a number of sub-tasks are usually clearly identifiable as separate activities—e.g.,

1.  Order-getting

    1.1  Advertising

    1.2  Outside selling

    1.3  House selling or order desk function.

2.  Order-filling

    2.1  Order processing and control

    2.2  Billing (invoice pricing, checking and typing)

3.  Shipping and delivery

    3.1  Warehousing of finished products

    3.2  Stock-pulling

    3.3  Packing

    3.4  Delivery or shipment

4.  Credit and collection

    4.1  Credit authorization

    4.2  Maintenance of accounts receivable records

    4.3  Collection of outstanding accounts

5.  Sales management

    5.1  District or territory management

    5.2  Maintenance of sales statistical and control records.

Figure 19 illustrates how this functional analysis may be constructed while Figure 20 indicates some of the possible bases for allocating distribution costs to customers or to products.

In practice, it is usually found that every item of expense can be related on a reasonably objective basis, either to the customers involved or to the products handled. Later, both customer and product costs can be re-combined in a meaningful manner in the analysis of a given segment of sales for a selected period—in order to provide answers for some of the questions that may have considerable significance to sales management.

## Figure 19.
### THE OLD-LINE MANUFACTURING COMPANY
### ANALYSIS OF DISTRIBUTION COSTS BY FUNCTION
(Monthly Budget)

| | TOTAL | ORDER-GETTING | ORDER-FILLING | SHIPPING | CREDIT | SALES MGT. | GENERAL ADMIN. |
|---|---|---|---|---|---|---|---|
| **SELLING EXPENSE:** | | | | | | | |
| Management salaries | $ 2,083 | | | | | $ 2,083 | |
| Salesmen's salaries | 14,275 | $14,275 | | | | | |
| Commissions | 13,500 | 13,500 | | | | | |
| Travel expense | 1,125 | 875 | | | $ 100 | 150 | |
| Advertising | 9,875 | 9,875 | | | | | |
| Other promotion ex. | 1,150 | 1,000 | | | | 150 | |
| Telephone & telegraph | 1,600 | 1,520 | | | | 80 | |
| Sales office rent | 1,500 | 1,200 | | | | 300 | |
| Warehouse salaries | 2,667 | | | $ 2,667 | | | |
| Freight out | 5,942 | | | 5,942 | | | |
| | $53,717 | | | | | | |
| **ADMINISTRATIVE EXPENSE:** | | | | | | | |
| Management salaries | $ 5,167 | | | | 1,000 | | $ 4,167 |
| Clerical salaries | 12,833 | | $ 2,000 | 558 | 1,375 | | 8,900 |
| Data Processing | 8,042 | | | | | 400 | 7,642 |
| Stationery | 1,525 | 217 | 208 | 83 | 142 | 50 | 825 |
| Bad debts | 1,350 | | | | 1,350 | | |
| Telephone & telegraph | 400 | | | | 50 | | 350 |
| Office rent | 500 | | 100 | | 100 | | 300 |
| Depreciation, office equipment | 258 | | 25 | | 50 | 33 | 150 |
| | $30,075 | | | | | | |
| | $83,792 | $42,462 | $ 2,333 | $ 9,250 | $ 4,167 | $ 3,246 | $22,334 |

## Figure 20.

### THE OLD-LINE MANUFACTURING COMPANY

Bases for allocating Distribution Costs
to Customers or to Products

| ORDER-GETTING: | CUSTOMER COSTS | PRODUCT COSTS | BASIS OF ALLOCATION |
|---|---|---|---|
| Advertising | | $ 9,875 | Actual per agency accounts |
| Commissions | | 13,500 | Actual @ 5% of the sales dollar |
| All other | $19,087 | | Number of calls x miles travelled |
| **ORDER-FILLING:** | | | |
| Stationery and supplies | 208 | | Number of invoices |
| All other | 2,125 | | Number of invoice lines |
| **SHIPPING AND DELIVERY:** | | | |
| Warehouse salaries | | 2,667 | Average inventory value of finished goods |
| Freight out, clerical salaries, stationery | | 6,583 | Standard unit weight x distance from shipping point to customer (cwt. per mile) |
| **CREDIT AND COLLECTIONS:** | | | |
| Bad debts | 1,350 | | Standard allowance (½ of 1% of sales) |
| All other | 2,817 | | Number of orders |
| **SALES MANAGEMENT:** | | | |
| Total cost of the function | 3,246 | | Number of calls x miles travelled |
| | $28,833 | $32,625 | |
| | | $61,458 | |
| **GENERAL ADMINISTRATION:** | | | |
| Not assigned except as a surcharge | | 22,334 | 8.272% of the sales dollar |
| **TOTAL**, as per monthly budget | | $83,792 | |

Figure 21 illustrates the type of schedule that would be employed to calculate certain costs that are specific to particular products or to particular customers. In practice, separate schedules would be required for each of the items under Order-Filling, Shipping and Delivery, and Credit and Collections, but the example of how Order-Getting costs are allocated is sufficient to illustrate the technique involved.

### Figure 21.

## THE OLD-LINE MANUFACTURING COMPANY

### Allocation of Order-Getting Costs

#### (1) TO PRODUCTS

| CHAIR MODEL: | SALES DOLLARS | COMMISSIONS @ 5% | ADVERTISING (ACTUAL) |
|---|---|---|---|
| D40 | $ 21,600 | $ 1,080 | — |
| D4A | 18,900 | 945 | — |
| D56 | 27,000 | 1,350 | — |
| D6E | 32,400 | 1,620 | $ 1,580 |
| D7A | 37,800 | 1,890 | 1,855 |
| D8A | 43,200 | 2,160 | 2,100 |
| D98 | 48,600 | 2,430 | 2,375 |
| DAA | 40,500 | 2,025 | 1,965 |
| | $270,000 | $ 13,500 | $ 9,875 |

#### (2) TO CUSTOMERS

| CUSTOMERS: | CALLS × MILES | % | ORDER-GETTING | SALES MANAGE-MENT |
|---|---|---|---|---|
| Baffin University | 2,020 | 29.1 | $ 5,554 | $ 945 |
| DRJ Store Equipment Co. | 150 | 2.2 | 420 | 71 |
| Hastings Auditorium | 320 | 4.6 | 878 | 149 |
| House of Forreste | 240 | 3.5 | 668 | 114 |
| Krausz Mfg. Ltd. | 144 | 2.1 | 401 | 68 |
| Novakino Theatres | 1,565 | 22.5 | 4,295 | 730 |
| Simcoe Airways | 1,080 | 15.5 | 2,959 | 503 |
| Swan Lake Studios | 25 | 0.4 | 76 | 13 |
| Trebolino Supply Co. | 980 | 14.1 | 2,691 | 458 |
| Miscellaneous | 416 | 6.0 | 1,145 | 195 |
| | 6,940 | 100.0 | $19,087 | $3,246 |
| | | | | $22,333 |

Finally, the results of this identification of the functional costs of distribution for specific products and specific customers may be brought together as illustrated by the following schedules:

## Figure 22.

### THE OLD-LINE MANUFACTURING COMPANY
### SALES AND (COST OF SALES) — PRODUCTS BY CUSTOMER
Month of June, 19—

| | D40 | D4A | D56 | D6E | D7A | D8A | D98 | DAA | TOTAL |
|---|---|---|---|---|---|---|---|---|---|
| Baffin University | — | — | — | — | — | — | — | $29,430 (17,658) | $ 29,430 (17,658) |
| DJR Store Equipment Co. | — | — | — | — | — | — | — | 11,070 (6,642) | 11,070 (6,642) |
| Hastings Auditorium | — | — | $27,000 (15,390) | $27,540 (15,973) | — | — | — | — | 54,540 (31,363) |
| House of Forreste | $ 8,400 (4,700) | $ 6,850 (3,768) | — | — | — | $ 5,000 (3,050) | $ 5,400 (3,348) | — | 25,650 (14,866) |
| Krausz Mfg. Ltd. | — | — | — | — | — | 21,870 (13,340) | — | — | 21,870 (13,340) |
| Novakino Theatres | — | — | — | — | $27,000 (14,850) | — | — | — | 27,000 (14,850) |
| Simcoe Airways | — | — | — | 4,860 (2,819) | — | — | 29,700 (18,414) | — | 34,560 (21,233) |
| Swan Lake Studios | — | — | — | — | 10,800 (5,900) | — | — | — | 10,800 (5,900) |
| Trebolino Supply Co. | 10,000 (5,600) | 5,450 (2,998) | — | — | — | 15,000 (9,150) | 6,000 (3,720) | — | 36,450 (21,468) |
| Miscellaneous | 3,200 (1,796) | 6,600 (3,630) | — | — | — | 1,330 (812) | 7,500 (4,650) | — | 18,630 (10,888) |
| TOTAL | $21,600 (12,096) | $18,900 (10,396) | $27,000 (15,390) | $32,400 (18,792) | $37,800 (20,750) | $43,200 (26,352) | $48,600 (30,132) | $40,500 (24,300) | $270,000 (158,208) |

## Figure 23.

### THE OLD-LINE MANUFACTURING COMPANY
### PROFIT & LOSS BY CUSTOMER
Month of June, 19——

| CUSTOMER | SALES | GROSS MARGIN | ORDER-GETTING | ORDER-FILLING | CREDIT | BAD DEBTS | TOTAL CUSTOMER EXPENSES | GROUP MARGIN |
|---|---|---|---|---|---|---|---|---|
| DRJ Store Equipment Co. | $ 11,070 100.0% | 4,428 40.0% | 491 4.4% | 550 5.0% | 256 2.3% | 55 0.5% | 1,352 12.2% | 3,076 27.8% |
| Baffin University | $ 29,430 100.0% | 11,772 40.0% | 6,499 22.1% | 127 0.4% | 127 0.4% | 147 0.5% | 6,900 23.4% | 4,872 16.6% |
| Hastings Auditorium | $ 54,540 100.0% | 23,177 42.5% | 1,027 1.9% | 90 0.1% | 256 0.5% | 273 0.5% | 1,646 3.0% | 21,531 39.5% |
| House of Forreste | $ 25,650 100.0% | 10,784 42.0% | 782 3.0% | 114 0.4% | 127 0.5% | 128 0.5% | 1,151 4.4% | 9,633 37.6% |
| Krausz Mfg. Ltd. | $ 21,870 100.0% | 8,530 39.0% | 469 2.1% | 386 1.8% | 127 0.6% | 110 0.5% | 1,092 5.0% | 7,438 34.0% |
| Novakino Theatres | $ 27,000 100.0% | 12,150 45.0% | 5,025 18.6% | 446 1.7% | 383 1.4% | 135 0.5% | 5,989 22.2% | 6,161 22.8% |
| Simcoe Airways | $ 34,560 100.0% | 13,327 38.6% | 3,462 10.0% | 39 0.1% | 769 2.3% | 173 0.5% | 4,443 12.9% | 8,884 25.7% |
| Swan Lake Studios | $ 10,800 100.0% | 4,900 45.4% | 89 0.8% | 58 0.5% | 127 1.2% | 54 0.5% | 328 3.0% | 4,572 42.4% |
| Trebolino Supply Co. | $ 36,450 100.0% | 14,982 41.1% | 3,149 8.6% | 64 0.2% | 127 0.3% | 182 0.5% | 3,522 9.6% | 11,460 31.5% |
| Miscellaneous | $ 18,630 100.0% | 7,742 41.6% | 1,340 7.2% | 459 2.5% | 518 2.8% | 93 0.5% | 2,410 13.0% | 5,332 28.6% |
| TOTAL | $270,000 100.0% | 111,792 41.4% | 22,333 8.3% | 2,333 0.9% | 2,817 1.0% | 1,350 0.5% | 28,833 10.7% | 82,959 30.7% |

## Figure 24.

## THE OLD-LINE MANUFACTURING COMPANY
### PROFIT & LOSS BY PRODUCT
Month of June 19—

| PRODUCT | SALES | GROSS MARGIN | ADVERTISING | COMMISSIONS | WAREHOUSING | SHIPPING | TOTAL PRODUCT EXPENSES | GROUP MARGIN |
|---|---|---|---|---|---|---|---|---|
| D40 | $ 21,600 100.0% | 9,504 44.0% | — | 1,080 5.0% | 216 1.0% | 527 2.4% | 1,823 8.4% | 7,681 35.6% |
| D4A | $ 18,900 100.0% | 8,504 45.0% | — | 945 5.0% | 189 1.0% | 461 2.4% | 1,595 8.4% | 6,909 36.6% |
| D56 | $ 27,000 100.0% | 11,610 43.0% | — | 1,350 5.0% | 269 1.0% | 658 2.4% | 2,277 8.4% | 9,333 34.6% |
| D6E | $ 32,400 100.0% | 13,608 42.0% | 1,580 4.9% | 1,620 5.0% | 323 1.0% | 790 2.4% | 4,313 13.3% | 9,295 28.7% |
| D7A | $ 37,800 100.0% | 17,050 45.0% | 1,855 4.9% | 1,890 5.0% | 379 1.0% | 922 2.4% | 5,046 13.3% | 12,004 31.7% |
| D8A | $ 43,200 100.0% | 16,848 39.0% | 2,100 4.9% | 2,160 5.0% | 432 1.0% | 1,053 2.4% | 5,745 13.3% | 11,103 25.7% |
| D98 | $ 48,600 100.0% | 18,468 38.0% | 2,375 4.9% | 2,430 5.0% | 485 1.0% | 1,185 2.4% | 6,475 13.3% | 11,993 24.7% |
| DAA | $ 40,500 100.0% | 16,200 40.0% | 1,965 4.9% | 2,025 5.0% | 374 0.9% | 987 2.4% | 5,351 13.2% | 10,849 26.8% |
| TOTAL | $270,000 100.0% | 111,792 41.4% | 9,875 3.7% | 13,500 5.0% | 2,667 1.0% | 6,583 2.4% | 32,625 12.1% | 79,167 29.3% |

In the last two schedules, the term "group margin" is used to indicate the apparent profit on the sales to each customer or on the sales of each product line before general administration, which, as noted in Figure 20, is not assigned except as a surcharge.

The schedules showing profit by customer and by product provide powerful analysis tools with which to pinpoint profitable or unprofitable sales.

Let us relate some of the product sales to the customers who bought the products in question. For example, we know that all the DAA model sales were attributable to only two customers, Baffin University and DRJ Store Equipment Company (see Figure 22):

| | | DOLLARS | % |
|---|---|---|---|
| Sales: | | | |
| Baffin University | $29,430 | | |
| DJR Store Equipment Company | 11,070 | $40,500 | 100.0 |
| Gross Margin | | $16,200 | 40.0 |
| Product Expenses | | $ 5,351 | 13.2 |
| Customer Expenses: | | | |
| DRJ Store Equipment Company | $ 1,352 | | |
| Baffin University | 6,900 | 8,252 | 20.4 |
| | | $13,603 | 33.6 |
| Margin before General Administration | | $ 2,597 | 6.4 |
| General Administration @ 8.272% of Sales | | 3,350 | 8.3 |
| *Apparent net loss on DAA Sales* | | $ (753) | (1.9) |

One conclusion that may be made concerning the unsatisfactory profit performance of DAA sales is that the chief cause is the high customer expenses incurred on behalf of Baffin University which, as the schedule of profit and loss by customer shows, is specifically attributable to the high order-getting costs associated with this account.

Based on the results of this analysis, it might also be concluded that the sales to Novakino Theatres were likewise unprofitable, since this account also exhibits an usually high order-getting cost ratio.

Let us determine if this conclusion is correct.

| | DOLLARS | % |
|---|---|---|
| Sales to Novakino Theatres (all D7A) | $27,000 | 100.0 |
| Gross Margin | $12,150 | 45.0 |
| Product Expenses (calculated @ 13.3% of sales) | $ 3,591 | 13.3 |
| Customer Expenses (per schedule) | 5,989 | 22.2 |
| | $ 9,580 | 35.5 |
| Margin before General Administration | $ 2,570 | 9.5 |
| General Administration @ 8.272% of sales | 2,233 | 8.3 |
| Apparent net profit on sales to Novakino | $ 337 | 1.2 |

Thus, the account just barely passes the profitability test. However it must be admitted that both segments of sales are making some contribution to the fixed costs and ultimate profit of the Company. Hence, they cannot be labelled as "unprofitable" unless the same volume could have been achieved at a higher margin through other channels.

•   •   •

The techniques illustrated in this Chapter are not intended to discount the usefulness of the Direct Costing approach previously outlined. The "gross margin" developed can just as well represent the contribution margin after all direct manufacturing costs have been deducted from sales. If Direct Costing were employed, then, the result would be a higher percentage margin (p/v ratio) than the gross margin percentages arrived at in the foregoing examples, and a larger pool of fixed costs to absorb. Other things being equal, it will usually be good strategy to push those products with the higher p/v ratios, although the cost of selling to specific customers should not be overlooked—as the micro-analysis of DAA and Novakino sales has demonstrated. In other words, it will always be more profitable to sell to certain customers than to others, and to sell certain products than others. This, in essence, is what Distribution Costing is designed to disclose.

## • REFERENCES

1. *Distribution Costs, Their Control and Analysis* by André Parent, M. Com., R.I.A., Special Study No 3 published by the Society of Industrial Accountants of Canada, Hamilton, Ontario, 1962, p. 9.
2. *Cost Accounting: A Managerial Emphasis* by Charles T. Horngren, Ph.D., C.P.A., Prentice-Hall Inc., Englewood Cliffs, N.J., U.S.A., p. 522.

## • QUESTIONS AND CASE PROBLEMS

8.01  Why should distribution costs be analyzed?

8.02  Is the sales dollar a good basis for cost assignment to Products and to Customers?

8.03  Name some of the items that make up the "general management overhead" of a business. Is there any objective basis for allocating such costs to specific products or specific customers?

8.04 The Sales Manager of THE OLD-LINE MANUFACTURING COMPANY has expressed the opinion that "as long as you get a good gross margin on sales, there is no need to worry about the cost of selling any particular customer." Do you agree with this statement?

8.05 You know from the analysis of Order-Filling and Credit & Collection expense that these average $2,333.08 and $2,816.00 respectively on a monthly basis. During the month of April in the current year, the number of orders processed totalled 800, while the number of invoices issued aggregated 799.

Calculate the per-unit cost to process and bill every order and the cost to collect it. Are these statistics useful, and what action would you take based on this information?

8.06 THE NEW-LINE SALES CORPORATION does not consider that Bad Debts represent a distribution cost that must be provided for in advance because the company's collection experience has been excellent over the past five years. If a credit loss does occur, it is simply charged to "Customer Costs" for the client company in question. Is this approach sound?

8.07 If the media advertising of THE OLD-LINE MANUFACTURING COMPANY is purely "institutional"—that is, designed to create a favourable image for the product in general without reference to any specific models sold by the Company—how would you allocate this cost to each type of chair sold?

8.08 Half way through the year it is decided to discontinue production of the D40 and D4A model chairs. However, there is still a substantial number of these models in inventory which will not be disposed of before Christmas.

What changes in the Company's distribution cost analysis procedures are required to reflect this decision?

8.09 MORECHROME MOTORS LIMITED is undecided as to what basis to use in compensating its new car salesmen. It is considering the following approaches:

— a flat percentage of the sales dollar.
— a percentage of the gross profit after deducting any overallowance granted on a used car traded in on a new car (an "overallowance" may be defined as the excess of the price allowed to the customer for the vehicle traded in over the value at which it is taken into used car inventory).

— a percentage of the net profit after deducting a fair share of all the dealership operating expenses.

Discuss these alternatives. Which one is the best approach, in your opinion?

8.10 If sales of the D40 chair can be increased to an average of $50,000 monthly by spending $15,000 per month on advertising for this model alone, should this promotional campaign be undertaken? (Refer to Figure 24 in developing your answer).

8.11 SELECTIVE SALES LIMITED decided on the basis of last year's operating results to drop product lines D and E. These results were as follows, expressed in thousands of dollars:

|  | A | B | C | D | E | TOTAL |
|---|---|---|---|---|---|---|
| Sales | $600 | $300 | $100 | $120 | $80 | $1200 |
| Variable direct expenses | $420 | $145 | $ 85 | $115 | $75 | $ 840 |
| Indirect expenses | 80 | 40 | 13 | 16 | 11 | 160 |
|  | $500 | $185 | $ 98 | $131 | $86 | $1000 |
| Operating profit/(loss) | $100 | $115 | $ 2 | $(11) | $ (6) | $ 200 |

Following this action, the company was chagrined to learn that profits did not increase by $17 as expected, being the sum of the losses previously experienced on products D and E. In fact, total operating profit declined by $10, and C, which had previously been profitable, became unprofitable.

Explain why profits have not increased by the sum of the losses previously experienced on the discontinued lines, and why C has become unprofitable. Were the assumptions made by SELECTIVE SALES LIMITED correct in dropping products D and E?

8.12 Following is a summary of the operations of the 3-N SALES COM-PANY for the year ending May 31:

|  | DOLLARS | % OF SALES |
|---|---|---|
| SALES | $630,000 | 100. |
| COST OF GOODS SOLD | 390,600 | 62. |
| GROSS MARGIN ON SALES | $239,400 | 38. |
| SELLING EXPENSES: |  |  |
| Commissions | $ 18,900 | 3.0 |
| Sales salaries | 17,640 | 2.8 |
| Travelling expense | 12,600 | 2.0 |
| Advertising | 64,260 | 10.2 |
|  | $113,400 | 18.0 |
| MERCHANDISING PROFIT | $126,000 | 20. |

The sales consist of a uniform product sold at a constant price throughout the year, and produced at a uniform factory cost per unit.

Three salesmen are employed by the Company, Neville, Newton and Norbert, although a considerable volume of business constitutes "House Sales" which are mail orders received without any direct solicitation by a representative of the Company. Neville is employed on a straight commission basis and receives 7½% on his gross sales; Newton is paid a salary of $7,200 plus 5% on sales, while Norbert receives a salary of $10,440 and a commission of 3% on sales.

Advertising is charged 50% to House Sales and the balance is then divided equally among the three salesmen.

Travelling expenses broken down by salesmen are as follows:

Neville, $6,130; Newton, $3,725; Norbert, $2,745.

An analysis of the sales for the year is as follows:

|        |          |
|--------|----------|
| Neville | $152,440 |
| Newton  | 108,380  |
| Norbert | 68,270   |
| House   | 300,910  |

Prepare an analytical statement showing the merchandising profit for house sales and for each of the three salesmen. Also, comment upon the appropriateness or otherwise of the compensation plans used to reward each man for his efforts on behalf of the Company.

Make all calculations to the nearest dollar only.

# NINE

## SOME MANAGEMENT PITFALLS

---

Despite the precision of the analytical or problem-solving tools of Cost Accounting, it is still possible to come to erroneous conclusions through the misuse (or failure to use) the techniques provided. In practice, this usually happens through not recognizing the need to apply the techniques in a different way, or to structure a report outside the usual format of the accounting statements normally produced. The number of times such erroneous conclusions are arrived at by otherwise rational accountants and businessmen indicates that certain pitfalls are not easy to identify. Some of the more subtle examples are considered below in the form of case problems.

- ### THE "SPECIAL ORDER" DILEMMA

Familiar to every small manufacturer is the problem of whether or not to accept special orders which will help to utilize excess capacity. The orders are "special" in the sense that they do not fit into the normal pricing structure that is presented to customers at large. The general pattern is for a large nation-wide department store, for example, to tender a substantial order at 20% to 25% below the usual wholesale price to the trade. If the initial order is accepted, the business may gradually increase with periodic pressure being exerted by the department store to grant further price concessions on the basis that "what you are losing on price you make up on volume" and "no sales costs are incurred when you deal with us." Eventually, the proportion of the manufacturer's output which is being taken by the department store reaches the point where the latter virtually "owns" the supplier; and, while the manufacturer may be selling more

111

than he ever did in the past, he is probably making less in terms of net profit than he previously earned on a much lower volume.

Armed with the foreknowledge that this is a typical pattern of how the relationship between himself and a giant customer is likely to develop, the more timid small manufacturer may run as fast as he can in the opposite direction at the first overtures from the giant. However, it is not a case of a once-in-a-lifetime decision that must be made when the initial order is accepted. At each price break in the negotiations, the manufacturer still has the opportunity of rejecting the business; and if his quality is high, he may develop a profitable long-run relationship with his oversize customer without losing a significant degree of independence. The point is, each price break and volume change that is proposed must be carefully assessed using the quantitative techniques of Cost Accounting. This will have the secondary benefit of placing the less tangible or qualitative factors of the problem in better perspective, so that the latter may be weighed with a minimum of guesswork.

To illustrate, TERREBONNE TEXTILES LIMITED, a small synthetic yarn sweater manufacturer is presently producing at the rate of 36,000 dozen garments per year, which represents only 60% of the practical capacity of the plant. Figure 25 displays the operating results at this level.

## Figure 25.

### TERREBONNE TEXTILES LIMITED

Statement of Profit & Loss

Year ended December 31, 19—

|  | DOLLARS | PER DOZ. |
|---|---|---|
| Sales, 36,000 dozen | $720,000 | 20.00 |
| Cost of Sales: |  |  |
| Variable manufacturing costs | $432,000 | 12.00 |
| Fixed overhead costs | 140,400 | 3.90 |
|  | $572,400 | 15.90 |
| Gross Margin | $147,600 | 4.10 |
| Variable selling expenses | $ 72,000 | 2.00 |
| Fixed selling and administrative expenses | 57,600 | 1.60 |
|  | $129,600 | 3.60 |
| Pre-tax profit | $ 18,000 | 0.50 |

A large department store will buy 1,000 dozen a month at $15.00. Should this order be accepted?

The first reaction of the president of TERREBONNE is that the order should be rejected because "$15.00 is below our present cost of sales."

It thus becomes the responsibility of the accounting manager of the company to demonstrate what the choice involves in terms of profits realized or foregone by reason of accepting or rejecting the order. This may be done by a comparative statement, as illustrated in Figure 26.

**Figure 26.**

TERREBONNE TEXTILES LIMITED
Comparative Statement of Profit & Loss
Year ending December 31, 19—

|  | (1) WITHOUT SPECIAL ORDER | (2) SPECIAL ORDER, ADDITIONAL REVENUE/ COSTS | (3) COMBINED (1 + 2) |
|---|---|---|---|
| Sales: |  |  |  |
| Normal, 36,000 dozen @ $20.00 | $720,000 |  |  |
| Special, 12,000 dozen @ $15.00 | — | $180,000 | $900,000 |
| Cost of Sales: |  |  |  |
| Variable manufacturing costs, 48,000 dozen @ $12.00 | $432,000 | $144,000 | $576,000 |
| Fixed overhead costs | 140,400 | — | 140,400 |
|  | $572,400 | $144,000 | $716,400 |
| Gross Margin | $147,600 | $ 36,000 | $183,600 |
| *Variable selling expense | $ 72,000 | — | $ 72,000 |
| Fixed selling and administrative expenses | $ 57,600 | — | $ 57,600 |
|  | $129,600 | — | $129,600 |
| Indicated pre-tax profit | $ 18,000 | $ 36,000 | $ 54,000 |

*No selling expense is involved
in accepting the special order.

This case illustrates once again that total costs are sometimes more relevant than unit costs. Clearly it would be advantageous to accept the special order for 1,000 dozen garments per month @ $15.00 unless there are qualitative factors which offset the immediate favourable effects on profits. For example, it may be prejudicial to the goodwill of the regular customers of TERREBONNE if they learn that the department store is getting a price concession which they do not receive.

Speculating about the strategy of the department store, the latter may offer a further "incentive" in the form of an offer to buy an additional 1,000 dozen sweaters per month if the price is cut to $13.50 per dozen (i.e., 24,000 dozen per annum @ $13.50). This is still above the variable manufacturing cost of $12.00 per dozen, but note that the contribution margin has been cut in half so that TERREBONNE would now earn only as much profit on the entire volume of 24,000 dozen as it did on the previous twelve:

|  | 12,000 DOZ. @ $15.00 | 24,000 DOZ. @ $13.50 |
|---|---|---|
| Sales | $180,000 | $324,000 |
| Variable manufacturing costs @ $12.00/doz. | 144,000 | 288,000 |
| Contribution Margin | $ 36,000 | $ 36,000 |

Obviously, at a price of $13.50 per dozen, the volume/price trade-off has reached the point where it is no longer advantageous for TERRE-BONNE to accept any more special orders. Within the range of $15.00 to $13.50 per dozen, however, there is still an opportunity to increase profits but management would no doubt wish to assess the situation very carefully — e.g., how permanent is this business, and is it wise to tie up so much plant capacity with one customer?

### • THE "SUNK COST" TRAP

The term "sunk cost" is generally considered to mean an outlay that has been frozen in a fixed asset or some other long-term investment. In other words, it is a past cost, and one which cannot be changed no matter what action is taken in the present or the future. It is the failure to recognize this basic attribute of sunk costs that causes fuzzy thinking with respect to current problems. Such doubtful reasoning often centres around equipment replacement decisions.

For example, let us assume that the production manager of our hypothetical company had purchased a new automatic knitting machine. The machine cost $30,000 and was expected to have a useful life of 10 years. Three months after the machine had been delivered and installed, specifications were received covering another machine which would perform the same operations as the machine recently acquired, and would do so at twice the rate of the first machine with an annual savings in direct labour of $12,000. This new and faster unit was priced at $45,000 and had the same useful life expectancy of 10 years. The production manager also learned that the maximum trade-in allowance on the first machine would be $6,000.

The accounting manager was then consulted about the desirability of replacing the first machine, and he agreed with the production manager that the "sunk cost" of the first machine should not influence their thinking in assessing the wisdom or otherwise of purchasing the second machine. Accordingly, the accounting manager undertook to prepare some figures in support of a recommendation to purchase the second machine.

When the president was asked for his approval covering this new investment, the latter argued that it just didn't make sense to practically give away the first machine in which the company had recently invested $30,000. He pointed out that this would appear to be profligate spending when the company had not started to get its money's worth out of the first machine. Besides which, he argued, it would be most embarrassing to have to recommend buying a new machine to the board of directors so soon after installing the first one.

The production manager and the accounting manager listened patiently to these arguments, realizing that it was not simply the president whom they had to convince, but also the board of directors who kept a watchful eye over investments of this magnitude. However, the accounting manager had done his homework carefully and the schedule he presented showed that the cost of the first machine did not have a direct bearing on the decision:

**Figure 27.**

MACHINE REPLACEMENT DECISION I

|  | KEEP MACHINE #1 | BUY MACHINE #2 |
|---|---|---|
| Cost of 1st machine | $30,000 | $ 30,000 |
| Cost of 2nd machine | — | 39,000 ($45,000 less $6,000 |
| Total investment in machinery | $30,000 | $ 69,000 trade-in allowance) |
| *Less* Savings in direct labour over 10 years | — | (120,000) |
| Net Cost | $30,000 | $(51,000) |
| Net Savings | — | 81,000 |

The accounting manager also pointed out that even if the first machine had cost $90,000, the net savings would still be the same. In the latter event, it might appear that $90,000 was "going to waste," but this was simply not relevant. The basic fact to be kept in view was that an investment of $39,000 would produce a cash savings of $120,000 over a 10-year period (see Figure 28.).

There are, of course, other factors that would influence the decision. In order to be able to make the investment in Machine #2, the company would have to find the cash or arrange some sort of acceptable financing. At the same time, tax considerations would have some bearing on the net savings to be generated — depreciation or capital cost allowance on the

## Figure 28.

### MACHINE REPLACEMENT DECISION II

| | KEEP MACHINE #1 | BUY MACHINE #2 |
|---|---|---|
| Cost of 1st machine | $90,000 | $ 90,000 |
| Cost of 2nd machine | — | 39,000 |
| Total investment in machinery | $90,000 | $ 129,000 |
| *Less* Savings in direct labour over 10 years | — | (120,000) |
| Net Cost | $90,000 | $ 9,000 |
| Net Savings | | 81,000 |

machines would normally reduce taxable income and thus increase the total cash flow generated by the additional investment in Machine #2.

There is also the potential criticism that the officers of the company should have deferred the investment in Machine #1 until a new and more efficient model was available. However, managers in government or industry are rarely favoured with this sort of omniscience. The state of the art in most branches of technology is changing with such rapidity that few people can predict the nature or timing of new developments. The point to be recognized is that the history of a problem is not directly relevant to its solution. Given the present situation, unfavourable though it may be, one should select the course of action which promises the best *future* results. This means that managers must have the courage to overcome the psychological impediments to choosing the logical and most objective course of action in any given circumstance. Such impediments usually take the form of well-intentioned but misdirected inclinations to get "one's money's worth," to avoid "back-tracking," or to avoid drawing attention to a potentially embarrassing situation.

● THE "RETURN ON INVESTMENT" RIDDLE

The confusion surrounding the machine replacement decision discussed in the preceding section is often equalled by the misconceptions attached to the determination of the rate of return on an investment. Theoretically, the concept is not hard to grasp. If you buy a 7% bond at par, you can be reasonably sure that the investment will yield a return of 7% to maturity. If you buy the bond at a premium, the rate of return will be somewhat less than 7%. Or, if the bond is purchased at a discount, the rate of return will be greater than 7%. In either case, the exact rate can be readily calculated once the purchase price is known.

Moving into the area of depreciable fixed assets, however, the proper investment base for measuring the rate of return is not always easy to find. This is perhaps attributable to the fact that the accounting treatment of fixed assets and related depreciation thereon does not always run parallel to the economist's thinking on such matters.

At this point, some definitions are necessary. For the benefit of non-accountants, "depreciation" may be defined as the systematic amortization or writing-off of the original cost of a capital asset over its useful life. While it is generally accepted that depreciation is a proper cost item to be taken into account when measuring the results of an operation, a department, or even an entire business, it is sometimes difficult to grasp that it is also a component of the cash flow of a business. This is because depreciation does not involve a cash outlay (or more precisely, a reduction in working capital) when it is recorded in the accounts. The cash outlay was made when the capital asset which is being depreciated was acquired. Hence, when calculating the return on a capital investment using one of the time-adjusted measurement techniques (such as the "discounted cash flow" method, for example), depreciation must be added back if it was deducted in determining the net income or net cash inflow produced by the investment.

There is another feature of such techniques that needs to be kept in view: the present value or annuity tables used automatically provide for the recovery of the principal sum invested in computing the rate of return. Hence, to deduct depreciation from the cash flow generated by the investment would have the effect of including a capital recovery factor twice in the calculations.

How do these concepts affect the investment base for measuring the rate of return? Returning to the example in the preceding section, if the decision to buy Machine #2 is carried out, the accounting treatment of the transaction on the books of the company would probably be as follows:

(a) The cost of Machine #1 ($30.000) would be removed from a fixed asset account termed Machinery and the difference between its book value (i.e., original cost less accumulated depreciation, if any) and the proceeds from disposal would be charged to a profit and loss account termed Loss on Disposal of Fixed Assets. In this case, the "loss" would be $24,000 (i.e., $30.000 less the $6,000 trade-in allowance, there being no accumulated depreciation to be taken into account).

(b) The purchase value of Machine #2 ($45,000) would be charged to Machinery account.

Implicit in these entries is the assumption that the investment base is $45,000 and, in fact, this is how the rate of return would be measured using the "accounting method of return." [1]

$$R = \frac{E - D}{I}$$

where R = average annual rate of return
     E = additional average annual earnings before depreciation
     D = additional average annual depreciation
     I = new investment

Applying this formula to the investment in Machine #2, an average annual rate of return of 16.7% is indicated, assuming straight-line depreciation of 10% or $4,500 per year on the machine — i.e.,

$$R = \frac{\$12,000 - \$4,500}{\$45,000} = 16.7\%$$

However, there is really no justification for this rough-and-ready approach when a much more precise technique is available in the "discounted cash flow" (DCF) method. What the DCF method involves is summarized rather succinctly in the following definition:

> The Discounted Cash Flow (DCF) rate of return is the *discount rate* expressed as a percentage, at which the present value of all income resulting from a project, whether present or future, capital or expense, equals the present value of the capital expenditure which generated them. This discount rate, the DCF rate of return, is the economic basis on which the project can be compared with other projects or with the minimum acceptable rate of return to determine its desirability. [2]

Using Machine #2 again as an example, a simple calculation of the return on investment rate, using the DCF method and ignoring the effect of income taxes, would be:

| | |
|---|---|
| Amount to be recovered | $39,000 |
| Cash income per year | $12,000 |
| Ratio of return to investment | .3077 |

From our knowledge that the machine has a useful life of 10 years, the indicated rate of return is between 28% and 29% by reference to the "capital recovery factor" tables for n = 10. [3] (See pages 122-125.)

Assuming a corporate tax rate of approximately 50%, some analysts would estimate the after-tax rate to be about half the above rate, or in the region of 14.5%. This is only a rough approximation, however. If an accurate rate of return is to be developed, the impact of depreciation on income taxes payable (or "capital cost allowance" as it is termed under Canadian income tax law) needs to be taken into account.

It should also be noted that we have shifted our investment base from the $45,000 used in the "accounting method of return" to $39,000 — the net additional outlay required to acquire Machine #2. Most businessmen would agree with the economic concept that a proper measure of return can only be developed if the net additional or incremental investment is compared to the net change in income which results from the additional investment. If this principle is accepted, then, the proper investment base is the cost of Machine #2 ($45,000) *less* the trade-in allowance for Machine #1 ($6,000), or $39,000.

To illustrate, a comparison for year 1 may be made as shown in Figure 29, assuming both machines fall into Class 8 (20% on the reducing balance basis) for capital cost allowance purposes.

### Figure 29.

#### INCREMENTAL CASH OUTFLOW/(INFLOW)

|  | KEEP MACHINE #1 | BUY MACHINE #2 |
|---|---|---|
| Capital investment | $30,000 | $39,000 |
| Capital cost allowance @ 20% (year 1 only) | $ 6,000 | $ 7,800 |
| Savings | | (12,000) |
| Income tax base | | $ (4,200) |
| Tax @ 52% | | 2,184 |
| Net income after tax and capital cost allowance | | $ (2,016) |
| *Add back* Capital cost allowance | (6,000) | (7,800) |
| True cash inflow | — | $ (9,816) |

Since the cash inflows vary from year to year because of the effect of capital cost allowances on income taxes, it is necessary to calculate the annual net cash inflow for each year of the machine's useful life (see Figure 30. on the next page).

## Figure 30.

| YEAR | (1) UNDEPRE- CIATED CAPITAL COST | (2) CAPITAL COST ALLOWANCE @ 20% | (3) TAXABLE INCOME $12,000 — (2) | (4) TAX PAYABLE @ 52% | (5) NET CASH INFLOW: $12,000 — (4) |
|---|---|---|---|---|---|
| 0 | $39,000 | | | | |
| 1 | 31,200 | $ 7,800 | $ 4,200 | $ 2,184 | $ 9,816 |
| 2 | 24,960 | 6,240 | 5,760 | 2,995 | 9,005 |
| 3 | 19,968 | 4,992 | 7,008 | 3,644 | 8,356 |
| 4 | 15,974 | 3,994 | 8,006 | 4,163 | 7,837 |
| 5 | 12,779 | 3,195 | 8,805 | 4,579 | 7,421 |
| 6 | 10,223 | 2,556 | 9,444 | 4,911 | 7,089 |
| 7 | 8,178 | 2,045 | 9,955 | 5,177 | 6,823 |
| 8 | 6,542 | 1,636 | 10,364 | 5,389 | 6,611 |
| 9 | 5,234 | 1,308 | 10,692 | 5,560 | 6,440 |
| 10 | 4,187 | 1,047 | 10,953 | 5,695 | 6,305 |
| | | $34,813 | $85,187 | $44,297 | $75,703 |

The next step is to find that rate at which the present value of the income (column 5 above) equals the present value of the capital expenditure ($39,000).

The ratio of the average annual return (1/10 of $75,703) to the investment is $\frac{7,570}{39,000} = .1941$ which indicates a rate of return of approximately 15% by reference to the "capital recovery factor" tables for 10 years. This provides a starting point, although we can assume that the true rate is higher since the distribution of cash inflows is skewed towards the beginning of the series (because of the higher capital cost allowances that may be claimed in the earlier years).

| | | INTEREST RATE — 15% | | INTEREST RATE — 16% | |
|---|---|---|---|---|---|
| YEAR | CASH FLOW ($'000) | PRESENT WORTH FACTOR | PRESENT WORTH ($'000) | PRESENT WORTH FACTOR | PRESENT WORTH ($'000) |
| 0 | (39.0) | 1.0000 | (39.0) | 1.0000 | (39.0) |
| 1 | 9.8 | .8696 | 8.5 | .8621 | 8.4 |
| 2 | 9.0 | .7561 | 6.8 | .7432 | 6.7 |
| 3 | 8.4 | .6575 | 5.5 | .6407 | 5.4 |
| 4 | 7.8 | .5718 | 4.5 | .5523 | 4.3 |
| 5 | 7.4 | .4972 | 3.7 | .4761 | 3.5 |
| 6 | 7.1 | .4323 | 3.1 | .4104 | 2.9 |
| 7 | 6.8 | .3759 | 2.6 | .3538 | 2.4 |
| 8 | 6.6 | .3269 | 2.2 | .3050 | 2.0 |
| 9 | 6.4 | .2843 | 1.8 | .2630 | 1.7 |
| 10 | 6.3 | .2472 | 1.6 | .2267 | 1.4 |
| | | | 1.3 | | (0.3) |

The actual rate, by interpolation, is 15.8%,

$$\text{i.e., } 15 + \frac{1.3}{1.3 - (-0.3)} \quad (16 - 15) = 15.812$$

In view of the apparent complexity of the DCF approach, some executives may well ask if such a refined method is necessary. The answer is that the DCF technique represents a more theoretically sound method of relating earnings to capital expenditure than any of the alternatives. At the same time, it should be emphasized that the results are still based on assumptions that may not apply over the lifespan of the capital asset or project involved — capital cost allowance rates and income tax rates may change, or the annual earnings may vary from the original forecast for a variety of reasons. However, this would be true regardless of what method was employed for measuring the rate of return, and as Dr. R. L. Martino observed in a recent book, "no matter how inaccurate our data, we always get a more nearly accurate answer when we use the right rule." [4]

● **REFERENCES**

1. This particular statement of the formula is taken from *Cost Accounting: A Managerial Emphasis* by C. T. Horngren, Ph.D., C.P.A., published by Prentice-Hall Inc., Englewood Cliffs, N.J., U.S.A., p. 373.

2. *The Appraisal of Capital Expenditure* by C. G. Edge, B.Sc. (Econ.), F.S.S., R.I.S., R.I.A., Special Study No. 1, Revised Edition, published by the Society of Industrial Accountants of Canada, Hamilton, Ontario, pp. 14-15.

3. *Ibid,* Table 6, p. 190. Edge defines the "capital recovery factors" as "the series of 'n' payments which will be yielded by a given sum invested now." The tables in this manual are synonymous with standard annuity tables, $a\frac{-1}{n|}$ although the factors are only taken to four decimal places (see, for example, *Compound Interest and Annuity Tables* published by the Financial Publishing Company, Boston, Mass., U.S.A.).

4. *Dynamic Costing* by R. L. Martino, Ph.D., published by the Management Development Institute Inc., Wayne, Penn., U.S.A., p. 27.

## CAPITAL RECOVERY FACTORS

Used to determine the series of 'n' payments which will be yielded by a given sum invested now

| Years | 1% | 2% | 3% | 4% | 5% | 6% | 7% | 8% | 9% | 10% |
|---|---|---|---|---|---|---|---|---|---|---|
| 1 | 1.0100 | 1.0200 | 1.0300 | 1.0400 | 1.0500 | 1.0600 | 1.0700 | 1.0800 | 1.0900 | 1.1000 |
| 2 | .5076 | .5155 | .5226 | .5305 | .5376 | .5455 | .5529 | .5606 | .5685 | .5760 |
| 3 | .3401 | .3466 | .3534 | .3604 | .3671 | .3741 | .3811 | .3880 | .3951 | .4021 |
| 4 | .2564 | .2625 | .2691 | .2755 | .2820 | .2886 | .2952 | .3019 | .3086 | .3155 |
| 5 | .2062 | .2121 | .2183 | .2246 | .2309 | .2374 | .2439 | .2505 | .2571 | .2638 |
| 6 | .1724 | .1786 | .1846 | .1907 | .1970 | .2034 | .2098 | .2163 | .2229 | .2296 |
| 7 | .1486 | .1546 | .1605 | .1666 | .1728 | .1792 | .1855 | .1921 | .1987 | .2054 |
| 8 | .1307 | .1365 | .1425 | .1485 | .1547 | .1610 | .1675 | .1740 | .1807 | .1874 |
| 9 | .1167 | .1225 | .1284 | .1345 | .1407 | .1470 | .1535 | .1601 | .1668 | .1736 |
| 10 | .1056 | .1113 | .1172 | .1233 | .1295 | .1359 | .1424 | .1490 | .1558 | .1627 |
| 11 | .0964 | .1022 | .1081 | .1142 | .1204 | .1268 | .1334 | .1401 | .1469 | .1540 |
| 12 | .0888 | .0946 | .1005 | .1066 | .1128 | .1193 | .1259 | .1327 | .1396 | .1468 |
| 13 | .0824 | .0881 | .0940 | .1002 | .1065 | .1130 | .1197 | .1265 | .1336 | .1408 |
| 14 | .0769 | .0826 | .0885 | .0947 | .1010 | .1076 | .1143 | .1213 | .1284 | .1357 |
| 15 | .0721 | .0778 | .0838 | .0899 | .0963 | .1030 | .1098 | .1168 | .1241 | .1315 |
| 16 | .0679 | .0736 | .0796 | .0858 | .0923 | .0989 | .1059 | .1130 | .1203 | .1278 |
| 17 | .0643 | .0700 | .0759 | .0822 | .0887 | .0955 | .1024 | .1096 | .1171 | .1247 |
| 18 | .0610 | .0667 | .0727 | .0790 | .0855 | .0924 | .0994 | .1067 | .1142 | .1219 |
| 19 | .0580 | .0638 | .0698 | .0761 | .0827 | .0896 | .0968 | .1041 | .1117 | .1195 |
| 20 | .0554 | .0612 | .0672 | .0736 | .0802 | .0872 | .0944 | .1018 | .1095 | .1175 |
| 21 | .0530 | .0588 | .0649 | .0713 | .0780 | .0850 | .0923 | .0998 | .1076 | .1156 |
| 22 | .0509 | .0566 | .0627 | .0692 | .0760 | .0830 | .0904 | .0980 | .1059 | .1140 |
| 23 | .0489 | .0547 | .0608 | .0673 | .0741 | .0813 | .0887 | .0964 | .1044 | .1126 |
| 24 | .0471 | .0529 | .0590 | .0656 | .0725 | .0797 | .0872 | .0950 | .1030 | .1113 |
| 25 | .0454 | .0512 | .0574 | .0640 | .0710 | .0782 | .0858 | .0937 | .1018 | .1102 |
| 26 | .0439 | .0497 | .0559 | .0626 | .0696 | .0769 | .0846 | .0925 | .1007 | .1092 |
| 27 | .0424 | .0483 | .0546 | .0612 | .0683 | .0757 | .0834 | .0914 | .0997 | .1083 |
| 28 | .0411 | .0470 | .0533 | .0600 | .0671 | .0746 | .0824 | .0905 | .0988 | .1074 |
| 29 | .0399 | .0458 | .0521 | .0589 | .0660 | .0736 | .0815 | .0896 | .0981 | .1067 |
| 30 | .0387 | .0447 | .0510 | .0578 | .0651 | .0726 | .0806 | .0888 | .0973 | .1061 |
| 31 | .0377 | .0436 | .0500 | .0569 | .0641 | .0718 | .0798 | .0881 | .0967 | .1055 |
| 32 | .0367 | .0426 | .0490 | .0560 | .0633 | .0710 | .0791 | .0875 | .0961 | .1050 |
| 33 | .0357 | .0417 | .0482 | .0551 | .0625 | .0703 | .0784 | .0869 | .0956 | .1045 |
| 34 | .0348 | .0408 | .0473 | .0543 | .0618 | .0696 | .0778 | .0863 | .0951 | .1041 |
| 35 | .0340 | .0400 | .0465 | .0536 | .0611 | .0690 | .0772 | .0858 | .0946 | .1037 |
| 36 | .0332 | .0392 | .0458 | .0529 | .0604 | .0684 | .0767 | .0853 | .0942 | .1033 |
| 37 | .0325 | .0385 | .0451 | .0522 | .0598 | .0679 | .0762 | .0849 | .0939 | .1030 |
| 38 | .0318 | .0378 | .0445 | .0516 | .0593 | .0674 | .0758 | .0845 | .0935 | .1027 |
| 39 | .0311 | .0372 | .0438 | .0511 | .0588 | .0669 | .0754 | .0842 | .0932 | .1025 |
| 40 | .0305 | .0366 | .0433 | .0505 | .0583 | .0665 | .0750 | .0839 | .0930 | .1023 |
| 41 | .0299 | .0360 | .0427 | .0500 | .0578 | .0661 | .0747 | .0836 | .0927 | .1021 |
| 42 | .0293 | .0354 | .0422 | .0495 | .0574 | .0657 | .0743 | .0833 | .0925 | .1019 |
| 43 | .0287 | .0349 | .0417 | .0491 | .0570 | .0653 | .0740 | .0830 | .0923 | .1017 |
| 44 | .0282 | .0344 | .0412 | .0487 | .0566 | .0650 | .0738 | .0828 | .0921 | .1015 |
| 45 | .0277 | .0339 | .0408 | .0483 | .0563 | .0647 | .0735 | .0826 | .0919 | .1014 |
| 46 | .0272 | .0335 | .0404 | .0479 | .0559 | .0644 | .0733 | .0824 | .0917 | .1013 |
| 47 | .0268 | .0330 | .0400 | .0475 | .0556 | .0642 | .0730 | .0822 | .0916 | .1011 |
| 48 | .0263 | .0326 | .0396 | .0472 | .0553 | .0639 | .0728 | .0820 | .0915 | .1010 |
| 49 | .0259 | .0322 | .0392 | .0469 | .0550 | .0637 | .0726 | .0819 | .0913 | .1009 |
| 50 | .0255 | .0318 | .0389 | .0465 | .0548 | .0634 | .0725 | .0817 | .0912 | .1009 |

## CAPITAL RECOVERY FACTORS

Used to determine the series of 'n' payments which will be yielded by a given sum invested now

| Years | 11% | 12% | 13% | 14% | 15% | 16% | 17% | 18% | 19% | 20% |
|---|---|---|---|---|---|---|---|---|---|---|
| 1 | 1.1100 | 1.1200 | 1.1300 | 1.1400 | 1.1500 | 1.1600 | 1.1700 | 1.1800 | 1.1900 | 1.2000 |
| 2 | .5839 | .5917 | .5994 | .6074 | .6150 | .6231 | .6308 | .6388 | .6467 | .6545 |
| 3 | .4092 | .4164 | .4236 | .4308 | .4380 | .4453 | .4526 | .4599 | .4673 | .4747 |
| 4 | .3223 | .3292 | .3362 | .3432 | .3503 | .3574 | .3646 | .3717 | .3790 | .3863 |
| 5 | .2706 | .2774 | .2843 | .2913 | .2983 | .3054 | .3126 | .3198 | .3270 | .3344 |
| 6 | .2364 | .2432 | .2501 | .2572 | .2642 | .2714 | .2786 | .2859 | .2933 | .3007 |
| 7 | .2122 | .2191 | .2261 | .2332 | .2403 | .2476 | .2549 | .2624 | .2698 | .2774 |
| 8 | .1943 | .2013 | .2084 | .2156 | .2228 | .2302 | .2377 | .2452 | .2529 | .2606 |
| 9 | .1806 | .1877 | .1949 | .2022 | .2096 | .2171 | .2247 | .2324 | .2402 | .2481 |
| 10 | .1698 | .1770 | .1843 | .1917 | .1993 | .2069 | .2146 | .2225 | .2305 | .2385 |
| 11 | .1611 | .1684 | .1758 | .1834 | .1911 | .1989 | .2068 | .2148 | .2229 | .2311 |
| 12 | .1540 | .1614 | .1690 | .1767 | .1845 | .1924 | .2005 | .2086 | .2169 | .2253 |
| 13 | .1481 | .1557 | .1634 | .1712 | .1791 | .1872 | .1954 | .2037 | .2121 | .2206 |
| 14 | .1432 | .1509 | .1587 | .1666 | .1747 | .1829 | .1912 | .1997 | .2082 | .2169 |
| 15 | .1391 | .1468 | .1547 | .1628 | .1710 | .1794 | .1878 | .1964 | .2051 | .2139 |
| 16 | .1355 | .1434 | .1514 | .1596 | .1680 | .1764 | .1850 | .1937 | .2025 | .2114 |
| 17 | .1325 | .1404 | .1486 | .1569 | .1654 | .1740 | .1827 | .1915 | .2004 | .2094 |
| 18 | .1298 | .1379 | .1462 | .1546 | .1632 | .1719 | .1807 | .1896 | .1987 | .2078 |
| 19 | .1276 | .1358 | .1441 | .1527 | .1613 | .1701 | .1791 | .1881 | .1972 | .2065 |
| 20 | .1256 | .1339 | .1424 | .1510 | .1598 | .1687 | .1777 | .1868 | .1960 | .2054 |
| 21 | .1238 | .1322 | .1408 | .1495 | .1584 | .1674 | .1765 | .1857 | .1951 | .2044 |
| 22 | .1223 | .1308 | .1395 | .1483 | .1573 | .1664 | .1755 | .1848 | .1942 | .2037 |
| 23 | .1210 | .1296 | .1383 | .1472 | .1563 | .1654 | .1747 | .1841 | .1935 | .2031 |
| 24 | .1198 | .1285 | .1373 | .1463 | .1554 | .1647 | .1740 | .1834 | .1930 | .2026 |
| 25 | .1187 | .1275 | .1364 | .1455 | .1547 | .1640 | .1734 | .1829 | .1925 | .2021 |
| 26 | .1178 | .1266 | .1357 | .1448 | .1541 | .1634 | .1729 | .1825 | .1921 | .2018 |
| 27 | .1170 | .1259 | .1350 | .1442 | .1535 | .1630 | .1725 | .1821 | .1917 | .2015 |
| 28 | .1163 | .1252 | .1344 | .1437 | .1531 | .1626 | .1721 | .1818 | .1915 | .2012 |
| 29 | .1156 | .1247 | .1339 | .1432 | .1527 | .1622 | .1718 | .1815 | .1912 | .2010 |
| 30 | .1150 | .1241 | .1334 | .1428 | .1523 | .1619 | .1715 | .1813 | .1910 | .2008 |
| 31 | .1145 | .1237 | .1330 | .1425 | .1520 | .1616 | .1713 | .1811 | .1909 | .2007 |
| 32 | .1140 | .1233 | .1327 | .1421 | .1517 | .1614 | .1711 | .1809 | .1907 | .2006 |
| 33 | .1136 | .1229 | .1323 | .1419 | .1515 | .1612 | .1710 | .1808 | .1906 | .2005 |
| 34 | .1133 | .1226 | .1321 | .1416 | .1513 | .1610 | .1708 | .1807 | .1905 | .2004 |
| 35 | .1129 | .1223 | .1318 | .1414 | .1511 | .1609 | .1707 | .1805 | .1904 | .2003 |
| 36 | .1126 | .1221 | .1316 | .1413 | .1510 | .1608 | .1706 | .1805 | .1904 | .2003 |
| 37 | .1124 | .1218 | .1314 | .1411 | .1509 | .1607 | .1705 | .1804 | .1903 | .2002 |
| 38 | .1121 | .1216 | .1313 | .1410 | .1507 | .1606 | .1704 | .1803 | .1902 | .2002 |
| 39 | .1119 | .1215 | .1311 | .1408 | .1506 | .1605 | .1704 | .1803 | .1902 | .2002 |
| 40 | .1117 | .1213 | .1310 | .1407 | .1506 | .1604 | .1703 | .1802 | .1902 | .2001 |
| 41 | .1116 | .1212 | .1309 | .1406 | .1505 | .1604 | .1703 | .1802 | .1902 | .2001 |
| 42 | .1114 | .1210 | .1308 | .1406 | .1504 | .1603 | .1702 | .1802 | .1901 | .2001 |
| 43 | .1112 | .1209 | .1307 | .1405 | .1504 | .1603 | .1702 | .1801 | .1901 | .2001 |
| 44 | .1111 | .1208 | .1306 | .1404 | .1503 | .1602 | .1702 | .1801 | .1901 | .2001 |
| 45 | .1110 | .1207 | .1305 | .1404 | .1503 | .1602 | .1702 | .1801 | .1901 | .2001 |
| 46 | .1109 | .1207 | .1305 | .1403 | .1502 | .1602 | .1801 | .1701 | .1901 | .2000 |
| 47 | .1108 | .1206 | .1304 | .1403 | .1502 | .1601 | .1701 | .1801 | .1901 | .2000 |
| 48 | .1107 | .1205 | .1304 | .1403 | .1502 | .1601 | .1701 | .1801 | .1900 | .2000 |
| 49 | .1107 | .1205 | .1303 | .1402 | .1502 | .1601 | .1701 | .1801 | .1900 | .2000 |
| 50 | .1106 | .1204 | .1303 | .1402 | .1501 | .1601 | .1701 | .1801 | .1900 | .2000 |

## CAPITAL RECOVERY FACTORS

Used to determine the series of 'n' payments which will be yielded by a given sum invested now

| Years | 21% | 22% | 23% | 24% | 25% | 26% | 27% | 28% | 29% | 30% |
|---|---|---|---|---|---|---|---|---|---|---|
| 1 | 1.2100 | 1.2200 | 1.2300 | 1.2400 | 1.2500 | 1.2600 | 1.2700 | 1.2800 | 1.2900 | 1.3000 |
| 2 | .6625 | .6705 | .6785 | .6865 | .6944 | .7025 | .7105 | .7187 | .7266 | .7348 |
| 3 | .4822 | .4897 | .4972 | .5047 | .5123 | .5199 | .5275 | .5352 | .5429 | .5507 |
| 4 | .3936 | .4010 | .4085 | .4159 | .4234 | .4310 | .4386 | .4462 | .4539 | .4616 |
| 5 | .3417 | .3492 | .3567 | .3642 | .3719 | .3795 | .3872 | .3949 | .4027 | .4106 |
| 6 | .3082 | .3158 | .3234 | .3311 | .3388 | .3466 | .3545 | .3624 | .3704 | .3784 |
| 7 | .2851 | .2928 | .3006 | .3084 | .3163 | .3243 | .3324 | .3405 | .3486 | .3569 |
| 8 | .2684 | .2763 | .2843 | .2923 | .3004 | .3086 | .3168 | .3251 | .3335 | .3419 |
| 9 | .2561 | .2641 | .2723 | .2805 | .2888 | .2971 | .3056 | .3140 | .3226 | .3312 |
| 10 | .2467 | .2549 | .2632 | .2716 | .2801 | .2886 | .2972 | .3059 | .3147 | .3235 |
| 11 | .2394 | .2478 | .2563 | .2648 | .2735 | .2822 | .2910 | .2999 | .3087 | .3177 |
| 12 | .2337 | .2423 | .2509 | .2597 | .2684 | .2773 | .2863 | .2953 | .3043 | .3134 |
| 13 | .2292 | .2379 | .2467 | .2556 | .2646 | .2736 | .2826 | .2918 | .3010 | .3102 |
| 14 | .2256 | .2345 | .2434 | .2524 | .2615 | .2706 | .2799 | .2891 | .2984 | .3078 |
| 15 | .2228 | .2317 | .2408 | .2499 | .2591 | .2684 | .2777 | .2871 | .2965 | .3060 |
| 16 | .2204 | .2295 | .2387 | .2479 | .2572 | .2666 | .2760 | .2855 | .2950 | .3046 |
| 17 | .2185 | .2277 | .2370 | .2464 | .2558 | .2652 | .2747 | .2843 | .2939 | .3035 |
| 18 | .2170 | .2263 | .2357 | .2451 | .2546 | .2641 | .2737 | .2833 | .2930 | .3027 |
| 19 | .2158 | .2252 | .2346 | .2441 | .2537 | .2633 | .2729 | .2826 | .2923 | .3021 |
| 20 | .2147 | .2242 | .2337 | .2433 | .2529 | .2626 | .2723 | .2820 | .2918 | .3016 |
| 21 | .2139 | .2234 | .2330 | .2426 | .2523 | .2620 | .2718 | .2816 | .2914 | .3012 |
| 22 | .2132 | .2228 | .2324 | .2421 | .2519 | .2616 | .2714 | .2812 | .2911 | .3009 |
| 23 | .2127 | .2223 | .2320 | .2417 | .2615 | .2613 | .2711 | .2810 | .2908 | .3007 |
| 24 | .2122 | .2219 | .2316 | .2414 | .2512 | .2610 | .2709 | .2808 | .2906 | .3005 |
| 25 | .2118 | .2215 | .2313 | .2411 | .2510 | .2608 | .2707 | .2806 | .2905 | .3004 |
| 26 | .2115 | .2213 | .2311 | .2409 | .2508 | .2607 | .2705 | .2804 | .2904 | .3003 |
| 27 | .2112 | .2210 | .2309 | .2407 | .2506 | .2605 | .2704 | .2804 | .2903 | .3002 |
| 28 | .2110 | .2208 | .2307 | .2406 | .2505 | .2604 | .2703 | .2803 | .2902 | .3002 |
| 29 | .2108 | .2207 | .2306 | .2405 | .2504 | .2603 | .2703 | .2802 | .2902 | .3002 |
| 30 | .2107 | .2206 | .2305 | .2404 | .2503 | .2603 | .2702 | .2802 | .2901 | .3001 |
| 31 | .2106 | .2205 | .2304 | .2403 | .2503 | .2602 | .2702 | .2801 | .2901 | .3001 |
| 32 | .2105 | .2204 | .2303 | .2402 | .2502 | .2602 | .2701 | .2801 | .2901 | .3001 |
| 33 | .2104 | .2203 | .2303 | .2402 | .2502 | .2601 | .2701 | .2801 | .2901 | .3001 |
| 34 | .2103 | .2203 | .2302 | .2402 | .2501 | .2601 | .2701 | .2801 | .2901 | .3000 |
| 35 | .2103 | .2202 | .2302 | .2401 | .2501 | .2601 | .2701 | .2801 | .2900 | .3000 |
| 36 | .2102 | .2202 | .2301 | .2401 | .2501 | .2601 | .2701 | .2800 | .2900 | .3000 |
| 37 | .2102 | .2201 | .2301 | .2401 | .2501 | .2601 | .2700 | .2800 | .2900 | .3000 |
| 38 | .2101 | .2201 | .2301 | .2401 | .2501 | .2601 | .2700 | .2800 | .2900 | .3000 |
| 39 | .2101 | .2201 | .2301 | .2400 | .2501 | .2600 | .2700 | .2800 | .2900 | |
| 40 | .2101 | .2201 | .2301 | .2400 | .2500 | .2600 | .2700 | .2800 | | |
| 41 | .2101 | .2201 | .2300 | .2400 | .2500 | .2600 | .2700 | .2800 | | |
| 42 | .2101 | .2200 | .2300 | .2400 | .2500 | .2600 | .2700 | | | |
| 43 | .2101 | .2200 | .2300 | .2400 | .2500 | .2600 | | | | |
| 44 | .2100 | .2200 | .2300 | .2400 | .2500 | | | | | |
| 45 | .2100 | .2200 | .2300 | .2400 | .2500 | | | | | |
| 46 | .2100 | .2200 | .2300 | .2400 | | | | | | |
| 47 | .2100 | .2200 | .2300 | .2400 | | | | | | |
| 48 | .2100 | .2200 | .2300 | | | | | | | |
| 49 | .2100 | .2200 | | | | | | | | |
| 50 | .2100 | .2200 | | | | | | | | |

## CAPITAL RECOVERY FACTORS

Used to determine the series of 'n' payments which will be yielded by a given sum invested now

| Years | 31% | 32% | 33% | 34% | 35% | 36% | 37% | 38% | 39% | 40% |
|---|---|---|---|---|---|---|---|---|---|---|
| 1 | 1.3100 | 1.3200 | 1.3300 | 1.3400 | 1.3500 | 1.3600 | 1.3700 | 1.3800 | 1.3900 | 1.4000 |
| 2 | .7429 | .7510 | .7591 | .7673 | .7755 | .7838 | .7920 | .8002 | .8085 | .8167 |
| 3 | .5584 | .5662 | .5740 | .5818 | .5896 | .5975 | .6055 | .6134 | .6214 | .6293 |
| 4 | .4694 | .4772 | .4850 | .4929 | .5008 | .5087 | .5167 | .5246 | .5327 | .5408 |
| 5 | .4185 | .4264 | .4344 | .4424 | .4505 | .4585 | .4667 | .4749 | .4831 | .4913 |
| 6 | .3865 | .3946 | .4028 | .4110 | .4193 | .4276 | .4359 | .4443 | .4528 | .4613 |
| 7 | .3651 | .3735 | .3819 | .3903 | .3988 | .4073 | .4159 | .4245 | .4332 | .4419 |
| 8 | .3504 | .3589 | .3675 | .3762 | .3849 | .3936 | .4024 | .4113 | .4202 | .4291 |
| 9 | .3399 | .3487 | .3575 | .3663 | .3752 | .3841 | .3931 | .4022 | .4112 | .4203 |
| 10 | .3323 | .3413 | .3502 | .3593 | .3683 | .3774 | .3866 | .3958 | .4050 | .4143 |
| 11 | .3268 | .3359 | .3450 | .3542 | .3634 | .3727 | .3820 | .3913 | .4007 | .4101 |
| 12 | .3226 | .3318 | .3411 | .3504 | .3598 | .3692 | .3787 | .3882 | .3976 | .4072 |
| 13 | .3196 | .3289 | .3383 | .3478 | .3572 | .3667 | .3763 | .3859 | .3955 | .4051 |
| 14 | .3172 | .3267 | .3362 | .3457 | .3553 | .3649 | .3746 | .3842 | .3939 | .4036 |
| 15 | .3155 | .3250 | .3347 | .3443 | .3539 | .3636 | .3733 | .3831 | .3928 | .4026 |
| 16 | .3142 | .3238 | .3335 | .3432 | .3529 | .3626 | .3724 | .3822 | .3920 | .4018 |
| 17 | .3132 | .3229 | .3326 | .3424 | .3521 | .3620 | .3717 | .3816 | .3914 | .4013 |
| 18 | .3124 | .3222 | .3320 | .3418 | .3516 | .3614 | .3713 | .3811 | .3911 | .4009 |
| 19 | .3118 | .3216 | .3315 | .3413 | .3512 | .3610 | .3709 | .3808 | .3907 | .4007 |
| 20 | .3114 | .3213 | .3311 | .3410 | .3509 | .3608 | 3707 | .3806 | .3905 | .4005 |
| 21 | .3111 | .3209 | .3308 | .3407 | .3506 | .3606 | .3705 | .3805 | .3904 | .4004 |
| 22 | .3108 | .3207 | .3306 | .3405 | .3505 | .3604 | .3704 | .3803 | .3903 | .4002 |
| 23 | .3106 | .3205 | .3305 | .3404 | .3504 | .3603 | .3703 | .3802 | .3902 | .4002 |
| 24 | .3105 | .3204 | .3304 | .3403 | .3502 | .3602 | .3702 | .3802 | .3902 | .4001 |
| 25 | .3104 | .3203 | .3303 | .3402 | .3502 | .3602 | .3701 | .3801 | .3901 | .4001 |
| 26 | .3103 | .3202 | .3302 | .3402 | .3501 | .3601 | .3701 | .3801 | .3901 | .4001 |
| 27 | .3102 | .3202 | .3302 | .3401 | .3501 | .3601 | .3701 | .3801 | .3900 | .4000 |
| 28 | .3102 | .3201 | .3301 | .3401 | .3501 | .3601 | .3700 | .3800 | .3900 | .4000 |
| 29 | .3101 | .3201 | .3301 | .3401 | .3501 | .3600 | .3700 | .3800 | .3900 | .4000 |
| 30 | .3101 | .3201 | .3301 | .3401 | .3500 | .3600 | .3700 | .3800 | .3900 | .4000 |
| 31 | .3101 | .3201 | .3300 | .3400 | .3500 | .3600 | .3700 | .3800 | .3900 | |
| 32 | .3101 | .3200 | .3300 | .3400 | .3500 | .3600 | .3700 | | | |
| 33 | .3100 | .3200 | .3300 | .3400 | .3500 | .3600 | | | | |
| 34 | .3100 | .3200 | .3300 | .3400 | .3500 | | | | | |
| 35 | .3100 | .3200 | .3300 | | | | | | | |
| 36 | .3100 | .3200 | .3300 | | | | | | | |
| 37 | .3100 | | | | | | | | | |

## • QUESTIONS AND CASE PROBLEMS

9.01 Discuss the implications of the following quotation: "We have one price to the trade and all buyers receive the same quotation regardless of the order size involved; we don't want to get the reputation of not treating *all* our customers fairly."

9.02 "As soon as a company commits itself to quoting prices below full product cost there is no turning back. A pattern of price cutting, once established, can only lead to bankruptcy."

Is this statement true or false? (Discuss).

9.03 "Depreciation is a cost but does not involve a cash outlay."

Explain this apparent paradox.

9.04 Which two methods of depreciation were referred to in this Chapter, and how would the annual allowance for depreciation be calculated under each method?

9.05 Following a period of exceptionally high earnings, THE PROFLIGATE COMPANY LTD. introduced a profit-sharing plan whereby all executives participate in a profit pool aggregating 20% of the net income of the Company before taxes. Shortly after the inception of the plan, the Vice-President, Finance (who is a participant in the plan) issued the following amendment to the Company's Accounting Procedures Manual:

> SPI-01-01-05-70:
>
> Effective immediately, office furniture and equipment, factory jigs and fixtures, fractional horse power motors, and all other items of durable tools and equipment, including improvements and betterments to existing machines, having a laid-down cost of $50 or more must be capitalized. This instruction replaces SPI-01-01-05-69.

SPI-01-01-05-69 specified a minimum cost of $100 for an item to be capitalized — i.e., charged to a depreciable fixed asset account.

It is estimated that this new policy will result in additions to depreciable fixed assets (subject to annual depreciation at a rate of 10% on a straight line basis) of $250,000 more in the current and subsequent years than in previous years when the "100 rule" was in effect.

(a) Calculate the amount that will be added to the executives' profit pool by this new policy, and the amount by which the share of the Vice-President, Finance will be increased if he participates to the extent of 4½%.

(b) Is this amendment to the Company's accounting procedures beneficial to the shareholders?

9.06 OLD-LINE INVESTMENTS LTD. is a holding company which owns the land and buildings used by THE OLD-LINE MANUFAC-TURING COMPANY in its operations. At a recent meeting of the Board of Directors of the former Company, it was decided to bring the fixed asset and accumulated depreciation reserves into agreement with the records of the District Taxation Office. Depreciation has been recorded on a straight line basis at a rate of 2½ % for the past five years but the maximum capital cost allowance has been claimed for tax purposes.

Details of the fixed asset and accumulated balances as shown by the records of OLD-LINE INVESTMENTS LTD. are as follows:

BUILDINGS, CLASS 3, 5%:

| YEAR | ASSETS | ACCUMULATED DEPRECIATION | NET BOOK VALUE |
|------|--------|--------------------------|----------------|
| 1965 | $330,000 | $41,250 | |
| 1967 | 75,000 | 5,625 | |
| 1969 | 110,000 | 2,750 | |
| | $515,000 | $49,625 | $465,375 |

(a) What is the amount of the adjustment required (to the nearest dollar) to convert the accumulated depreciation as at January 1, 1970, to the amount that would have been accumulated if the maximum capital cost allowance had been recorded each year up to and including 1969? (Use the formulae in Appendix A to make the calculations, and assume the reduced capital cost allowances imposed on additions made between March 29, 1966 and October 1, 1967 do not apply in this case).

(b) By how much will the 1970 capital cost allowance (to the nearest dollar) exceed depreciation calculated on a straight line basis, assuming there are no additions or disposals in 1970?

(c) If capital cost allowance (or depreciation) on buildings is reflected each year by an exactly equivalent rental charge from OLD-LINE INVESTMENTS LTD. to THE OLD-LINE MANUFACTURING COMPANY, by how much will the average unit cost per chair be increased in 1970 as a result of the revised depreciation policy, assuming the operating company plans to produce 175,000 chairs?

9.07    The President of TERREBONNE TEXTILES LIMITED remarked to his Accounting Manager in a half-humourous vein, "now that you talked me into buying that new knitting machine when the old one was less than six months old, I suppose you are going to tell me we should replace our company cars with new models every year?"

Does it follow from the replacement decision with regard to the knitting machine that the fleet of company cars should be traded in every year?

9.08    If an investment of $10,000 has a useful life of only four years during which time it generates a cash income of $3,019 each year, can we say that there has been no return on the investment until the 4th year, by which date the entire original cost has been recovered and some excess is received?

9.09    A construction company wishes to replace an equipment shed used for housing its road-building machinery during the winter months. A frame structure having a useful life of 10 years and costing $2,400 a year for maintenance can be erected for $36,000. A sheet metal building has a capital cost of $50,000 but its useful life is 15 years, and annual maintenance costs are only $1,200.

Which type of building should the construction company buy? (Hint: use the Capital Recovery Factor tables to convert total capital cost into equivalent annual costs, assuming an annual rate of return of 10%.)

9.10    The President of TERREBONNE TEXTILES LIMITED, who is the beneficial owner of all the issued and outstanding shares of the Company, has been negotiating with INTERNATIONAL CONGLOMERATE CORPORATION for the sale of these shares. The President of TERREBONNE wishes to obtain a price equivalent to five times annual earnings before taxes. ICC, on the other hand, requires a minimum return of 16% on a pre-tax basis for all investments. Both parties agree that $50,000 is an acceptable figure for average annual earnings before taxes, and that such earnings should continue at this level for the next ten years.

Is the selling price suggested by the President of TERREBONNE acceptable to ICC? If not, what is the maximum price ICC will pay for the shares of TERREBONNE?

9.11    "No matter how inaccurate our data, we always get a more nearly accurate answer when we use the right rule."

Show that this principle is correct by calculating the rate of return that would be earned by a purchaser of the depreciable fixed assets of TERREBONNE TEXTILES LIMITED over a 10-year period, assuming that the purchase price is $370,000 representing the current appraised value of these assets. That is, calculate the return on investment using (a) the "accounting method of return" assuming straight line depreciation of 10% per annum, and (b) the "discounted cash flow method" ignoring the impact of depreciation (or capital cost allowances) and income taxes on annual earnings. Again, as in problem 9.10, the figure of $50,000 may be taken as a reasonable index of pre-tax profit, provided allowance is made for the fact that it includes depreciation of $15,490 per annum calculated on the capital cost of the assets to the vendor company.

9.12 An explosion in the DISTILLATION DEPARTMENT of the chemical company (referred to in problem 4.10 above) has completely wrecked the equipment involved, including the computer used to monitor the operation. The book value of the equipment destroyed was $688,512 ($860,640 cost less accumulated depreciation of $172,128).

The company can replace the equipment configuration for $994,000 or subcontract the whole process to an outside laboratory for $10,800 per month, this price being guaranteed for at least three years. However, an initial programming fee of $30,000 is involved if this option is exercised.

Assuming the useful life of the replacement equipment, if purchased by the company, is seven years, and the labour required to operate the DISTILLATION DEPARTMENT is $1,600 per month, a cost which is expected to increase at the rate of 10% per annum for the forseeable future, which alternative should the company choose? (Discuss fully.)

9.13 The BISCUIT DIVISION of a packaged food company sells two-thirds of its production to the SALES DIVISION at retail less 30%, which represents a price of 41¢ per lb. The Manager of the SALES DIVISION has received an offer from an outside supplier for a similar product at 35¢ a lb. with guaranteed delivery of up to 100,000 lbs. monthly. A typical month's operating results for the BISCUIT DIVISION is shown by the schedule on the next page.

Assuming that the BISCUIT DIVISION cannot increase its sales to outside customers, is it advantageous to meet the price of 35¢ a lb. quoted to the SALES DIVISION, or should production be cut back forcing the SALES DIVISION to purchase all its requirements from outside sources?

|  | SALES DIVISION | OUTSIDE CUSTOMERS |
|---|---|---|
| SALES — 80,000 lbs. @ 41¢ | $32,800 | — |
| — 40,000 lbs. @ 59¢ | — | $23,600 |
| VARIABLE COST OF SALES | | |
| — 120,000 lbs. @ 25¢ | 20,000 | 10,000 |
| FIXED COSTS | 8,000 | 4,000 |
|  | $28,000 | $14,000 |
| GROSS MARGIN | $ 4,800 | $ 9,600 |

9.14  The MINI-RADIO CORPORATION (as may be recalled from problem 5.11) has the following unit costs covering the production and distribution of its portable AM/FM battery-powered radios at a level of 100,000 units per year:

Variable Manufacturing Cost per unit .................. $10
Fixed Manufacturing Costs per unit .................. $ 6
Fixed Selling and Administrative Costs per unit .... 80¢

Unfortunately, sales fell short of this "normal" level by 40,000 units last year with the result that the Company lost money. The Management Committee is considering what action should be taken in the current year to counter this unfavourable trend, and the following proposals have been put forward:

(a)  Reduce selling prices from the regular $20 per radio to $17.50 per unit, at which price the Sales Manager is confident the Company can sell at least 80,000 units.

(b)  Raise selling prices to $25 per radio. This will reduce the volume that the Company can reasonably hope to sell to 40,000 units, but the profit margin will be much improved.

(c)  Leave selling prices unchanged but spend $150,000 on a promotional campaign which will virtually assure that 75,000 units can be sold in the current year.

(d)  Produce a lower quality AM-only unit for the export market which will absorb 40,000 of these radios at a selling price of $12 per unit. Variable manufacturing costs for this "utility model" can be reduced to $8 per unit, and sales of the quality radio in the domestic market should remain unchanged at last year's level.

Which course of action do you recommend? Prepare relevant schedules to support your answer, including one showing the loss experienced last year.

# TEN

## THE FUTURE OF
## COST ACCOUNTING

---

Speculating about the future, all the evidence suggests that more and better cost data will be an essential ingredient of many business decisions. In fact, the growing use of quantitative methods as an aid to decision-making points to a greater importance for Cost Accounting than was envisaged in the past. If one examines the input data to the mathematical models or some of the common algorithms of operations research, for example, it soon becomes evident that they are entirely dependent upon accurate cost figures for the validity of the solutions they develop. An appreciation of the role of Cost Accounting in this context, then, requires some understanding of what is involved in the decision-making process itself, and how this process has been affected by operations research, management science, or whatever one may choose to call the collection of quantitative techniques that have been applied to business problems in recent years.

Operations research (or OR, to use the familiar abbreviation) evolved during World War II as a new approach to some urgent wartime strategic and tactical problems. Some six years later, or by 1951, OR was recognized as having a definite contribution to make in the solution of executive type problems within a business organization, and has since developed quite rapidly.

It has been said that OR is simply "the application of scientific method to management" [1] although the whole thing is perhaps put into better perspective by the following rather whimsical definition:

> ". . . the art of giving bad answers to problems to which
> otherwise worse answers are given." [2]

Management science is considered to encompass OR but also implies the use of electronic data processing or computer technology. The rapid development of electronic data processing during the 1960's has given

131

considerable impetus to OR. This is because, in the case of many of the mathematical models of OR, performing the calculations manually would take far too long and would significantly increase the incidence of error. By contrast, the same calculations can be made by a computer in a fraction of a second, in most cases, and with virtually 100% accuracy.

Within the limitations of this modest book, it would not be practical to attempt an explanation of all the numerous applications of OR that are now within the reach of the decision-maker. Accordingly, the examples below are restricted to two important techniques, probability theory and linear programming.

Considering linear programming first, this technique has been used to solve an impressive variety of business problems during the last 15 years or so. Some of the better known areas where the application of linear programming has produced results of significant value are:

(1) fixing economic order points and quantities to minimize inventory costs;
(2) selecting factory and store sites in such a way as to meet customer demand with maximum profit;
(3) determining the number of trucks required to cover a given territory at least cost;
(4) choosing the best product mix in order to maximize profit under conditions of limited machine capacities;
(5) determining how to ship at lowest cost and yet meet all requirements of availability and demand.

As a generalization, it may be stated that linear programming can often be used to find the optimum or best alternative within a set whenever alternative solutions are available.

This process of choosing between alternate courses of action is, in fact, a reasonably good definition for the decision-making process itself. It is somewhat of an over-simplification, of course, since all the alternatives are seldom equally well defined, and each alternative probably has a different degree of uncertainty associated with its outcome. But the difference between decision-making today and in the not-too-distant past is that there are now available a number of techniques to quantify some of the intangible or subjective data on which a decision is based. More precisely, some of the assumptions which were (presumably) implicit in arriving at a decision in the pre-management science era can now be explicitly stated, and even assigned weights to indicate their probable validity or chance of occurrence. At the same time, more systematic approaches have evolved which force consideration of all, not just some of the alternatives (for example, decision tables in the documentation of a computer system).

## ● PROBABILITY THEORY

The mathematics of probability have been used for years, if not centuries, by statisticians, actuaries and scientists. Hence, one can only wonder why the appearance of probability theory on the business scene was so long delayed.

Reduced to its simplest terms, probability theory states that, for any event which may or may not occur, the probability lies between the two extreme values of 0 and 1. If a particular event would never occur, $p = 0$. If a certain outcome will always occur, $p = 1$. This enables one to express the degree of probability for any particular event in quantitive terms rather than by such ambiguous phrases as "improbable," "more probable than not," or "highly probable." For a symmetrical coin, for example, the probability of getting either a head or a tail on any single toss is equal so that we may say that the probability of heads (or tails) is ½ (or 0.5).

In a practical accounting situation, probability assignments can give formal expression to the intuition or experienced judgment of managers. This can be particularly useful in the area of budgeting or forecasting, where it is often desirable to give an explicit measure of the degree of uncertainty that attaches to the figures involved.

As an illustration of this technique, let us turn once again to THE OLD-LINE MANUFACTURING COMPANY where the preparation of an annual sales forecast is the first step in the overall budgeting process.

Starting with the economy model, the D40 chair which sells at $12.50 per unit and has a variable manufacturing cost of $7.00, the following relevant information has been collected:

- Sales in the preceding fiscal year totalled 20,736 units for this particular model.
- The Vice-President, Sales, confidently expects an increase of 25% in company sales for the next fiscal year which will apply to all products across the board.
- A recent market survey conducted on behalf of the company concluded that the cheaper D40 and D4A chairs were gradually declining in customer preference in favour of the more de luxe models. Thus, sales of the cheaper lines were predicted to decline at the rate of 20% per year over the next few years unless a deliberate sales promotion campaign was undertaken to counter this trend.
- The Vice-President, Administration, reported that the 10-year trend of sales for all products showed an annual increase of approximately 10% on the basis of dollars (not necessarily units sold).

In evaluating these estimates, the President kept in view the record of the Vice-President, Sales, for being consistently over-optimistic. Hence, he concluded that there was only a 50:50 chance that the forecast of an overall increase in sales of 25% would be realized.

The market survey was based on fairly objective data, although its conclusions did not seem to be compatible with past sales performance. As a result, the President was convinced there was only a 60% chance that the predictions of the survey would be realized.

The evidence of the Vice-President, Administration based on long-term trends was the most tangible factor in the whole problem, the President felt, and any forecast based on this data should be right 9 times out of 10.

Summing up, what all these estimates amount to, as related specifically to D40 chairs, is an increase of 25%, a decline of 20% and an increase of 10% in next year's sales. And if the President's subjective appraisal of these estimates is to be used to supply weights for each estimate in the final sales forecast, his own weighting of each estimate must be scaled down since these weights add to 200%—i.e.,

| EVENT | WEIGHTING BY PERCENT CHANCE OF OCCURRENCE | PROBABILITY |
|---|---|---|
| Sales = 125% of last year | 50% | .25 |
| Sales = 80% of last year | 60% | .30 |
| Sales = 110% of last year | 90% | .45 |
| | 200% | 1.00 |

These estimates may now be converted into a dollar budget for the year, calcuated as follows:

## Figure 32.

### EXPECTED SALES OF D40 CHAIRS
Year ending December 31, 19—

(Note: previous year's sales = 20,736 units @ $12.50 or $259,200)

| EVENT | GROSS EXPECTED VALUES | PROBABILITY | EXPECTED VALUE WEIGHTED BY PROBABILITY |
|---|---|---|---|
| Sales = 125% of $259,200 | $324,000 | .25 | $ 81,000 |
| Sales = 80% of 259,200 | 207,360 | .30 | 62,208 |
| Sales = 110% of 259,200 | 285,120 | .45 | 128,304 |
| Most probable sales volume | | 1.00 | $271,512 |

Number of units @ $12.50 each = 21,720, or ($) rounded: $271,500

If sales are spread evenly throughout the year, monthly production of 1,810 units is required (1/12 of 21,700) assuming a safety stock of one month's sales is maintained).

## • LINEAR PROGRAMMING

Linear programming is perhaps best explained by analyzing the derivation of the words. A problem is "linear" if effects are proportional to causes. For example, the number of units and their cost are related linearly if, when the number of units produced is doubled, the cost also doubles. Mathematically, it may be recalled that a linear equation is one that can be represented by a straight line on a graph, and is of the general form $y = ax + b$.

"Programming" in this context means simply planning—planning of activities for the sake of optimization. In general, it is a decision-making process of choosing from a number of possible courses of action, the one which produces, for example, either maximum profit or least cost.

## • THE TRANSPORTATION PROBLEM

The transportation problem is a variation of the general linear programming problem. There is a fairly simple technique that may be used to solve this problem. The solution is arrived at through a series of tables rather than complicated mathematical equations, which makes it a good introduction to linear programming. The essential feature of the transportation problem is the determination of the optimum way of distributing a commodity from a number of shipping points to a number of destinations. "Optimum" in this context means that the total transportation costs are kept to a minimum. In other words, it is example #5 cited above on page 132—"determining how to ship at lowest cost and yet meet all requirements of availability and demand."

THE OLD-LINE MANUFACTURING COMPANY, as we have seen in a previous Chapter, has developed distribution costs covering most of the usual functions involved in getting its product into the hands of the customer. Hence, it is able to use the technique of the transportation problem to provide the answer to this frequently encountered question.

For purposes of example, let us assume that during the current week, the company has four customers to satisfy from stock available at three branch warehouses. For the sake of simplicity in calculations, the number of stock locations and the number of customers has been kept to a minimum in this illustration. However, it should be recognized that there is no real limitation on the quantities involved other than computational time.

Branch warehouse stocks are:

$$W_1 = 300 \text{ chairs}$$

$$W_2 = 400 \text{ chairs}$$

$$W_3 = 500 \text{ chairs}$$

... and customers' order requirements are:

$$C_1 = 200 \text{ chairs}$$

$$C_2 = 300 \text{ chairs}$$

$$C_3 = 400 \text{ chairs}$$

$$C_4 = 300 \text{ chairs}$$

It will be noted that sum of the warehouse capacities exactly equals the sum of customer demands. In any transportation problem, it is essential that the supply be at least as large as the demand, else there is no feasible solution. A more realistic set of warehouse capacities would be one whose total was greater than the customer demands. However, in this problem, the values have been deliberately chosen to reduce the amount of computation.

The costs of transporting one chair from any warehouse to any customer

**Figure 33.**

| | $C_1$ | $C_2$ | $C_3$ | $C_4$ | TOTAL |
|---|---|---|---|---|---|
| $W_1$ | .05 | .10 | .15 | .20 | 300 |
| $W_2$ | .20 | .15 | .10 | nil | 400 |
| $W_3$ | nil | .10 | .10 | .05 | 500 |
| TOTAL | 200 | 300 | 400 | 300 | 1,200 |

are shown below in the upper right-hand corner of each square (Figure 33). A "nil" cost means that the customer is located in the same city as the company's warehouse and uses his own truck to pick up orders.

Rather than use the "north-west corner rule," for example to obtain an initial feasible solution, we may make an immediate attempt at an optimum solution. This may be done by inspection in view of the simplicity of the problem (bearing in mind that the object of the exercise is to demonstrate the relevance of cost data, not to teach all the refinements of the transportation problem). That is, we will select the minimum cost (minimum $C_{ij}$, where $i = $ row, $j = $ column) for the maximum source quantity to be allocated, and proceed on this basis until the stock of each warehouse has been completely assigned to one or more customers.

This requires a start with $W_3$ from which we can immediately allocate 200 chairs to $C_1$ at zero cost.

The next largest quantity unassigned is $W_2$ with 400 chairs from which 300 chairs can be allocated to $C_4$ on the same zero cost basis.

If we had started with $W_1$, it would have been advantageous to allocate 200 chairs to the least cost customer, $C_1$, but since this demand has already been filled from $W_3$ at a more favourable cost (zero), we choose the next best allocation, $C_2$.

## Figure 34.

| | $C_1$ | $C_2$ | $C_3$ | $C_4$ | TOTAL |
|---|---|---|---|---|---|
| $W_1$ | .05 | .10 / 300 | .15 | .20 | 300 |
| $W_2$ | .20 | .15 | .10 / 100 | nil / 300 | 400 |
| $W_3$ | nil / 200 | .10 | .10 / 300 | .05 | 500 |
| TOTAL | 200 | 300 | 400 | 300 | 1,200 |

This only leaves $C_3$ demand to be satisfied from the residual supply of $W_2$ and $W_3$, so we assign 100 chairs from $W_2$ and 300 chairs from $W_3$ to complete the matrix, as shown in Figure 34.

The value of the "objective function," so-called, or the total transportation costs which this solution produces is:

$Z_0 = (300 \times .10) + (100 \times .10) + (300 \times 0) + (200 \times 0) + (300 \times .10) = \$70.00$

In order to prove that this is a "minimum feasible solution," *shadow costs* $U_i$ and $V_j$ may be introduced, such that $U_i + V_j = C_{ij}$.

From the preceding table, it can be stated that:

$$U_1 + V_1 = C_{11} = .05$$
$$U_1 + V_2 = C_{12} = .10$$
$$U_2 + V_3 = C_{23} = .10$$
$$U_2 + V_4 = C_{24} = 0$$
$$U_3 + V_1 = C_{31} = 0$$
$$U_3 + V_3 = C_{33} = .10$$

Arbitrarily let any one of these shadow costs equal its $C_{ij}$. For example, let $U_1 = .05$. This enables us to solve for the remaining shadow costs:

| | |
|---|---|
| $U_1 = .05$ (given) | $V_1 = 0$ |
| $U_2 = 0$ | $V_2 = .05$ |
| $U_3 = 0$ | $V_3 = .10$ |
| | $V_4 = 0$ |

Substituting the values of $C'_{ij} = U_i + V_j$ in a new cost table for *routes not used,* we have:

### Figure 35.

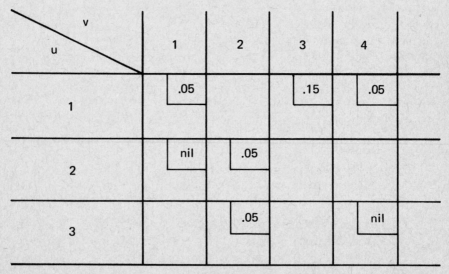

| u \ v | 1 | 2 | 3 | 4 |
|---|---|---|---|---|
| 1 | .05 | | .15 | .05 |
| 2 | nil | .05 | | |
| 3 | | .05 | | nil |

The original costs in the table for the minimum feasible solution are new subtracted from these new costs ($C'_{ij}$) for routes not used to ascertain if any alternative routes would produce lower costs:

$$C'_{11} - C_{11} = .05 - .05 = \quad 0$$
$$C'_{13} - C_{13} = .15 - .15 = \quad 0$$
$$C'_{14} - C_{14} = .05 - .20 = -.15$$
$$C'_{21} - C_{21} = \quad 0 - .20 = -.20$$
$$C'_{22} - C_{22} = .05 - .15 = -.10$$
$$C'_{32} - C_{32} = .05 - .10 = -.05$$
$$C'_{34} - C_{34} = \quad 0 - .05 = -.05$$

Since all $C'_{ij} - C_{ij} \leqq 0$, the solution ($Z_0 = \$70.00$) is a minimum feasible one.

It should be noted that the highest value for the objective function in this case is $180.00, which reveals a considerable spread between the highest cost and the lowest cost solution. This should demonstrate to the skeptical that a planned approach can be quite rewarding as compared to the results that might be produced by a random or haphazard solution.

• • •

The above simple examples are sufficient to illustrate that Cost Accounting has acquired a new dimension with the advent of operations research. Today, most OR practitioners will admit that the difficulty of acquiring accurate data for use in a model is often a more severe limitation to the application of OR to business problems than the ability to construct mathematical models or the limitations of computing facilities. Hence, a company which is producing relevant costs on a regular basis will have a headstart in the application of certain of the more sophisticated decision tools.

• REFERENCES

1. *Operational Research for Management* by M. J. Sargeaunt, M.A., A.M.I.EE., published by William Heinemann Ltd., London, Eng. p. 1.

2. *Mathematical Methods of Operations Research* by T. L. Saaty, McGraw-Hill Book Company Inc., New York, N.Y., U.S.A. 1959, p. 3.

## • QUESTIONS AND CASE PROBLEMS

10.01   What does OR (Operations Research) have to offer the business manager?

10.02   Why is Cost Accounting relevant to Operations Research?

10.03   What is a simple definition of the decision-making process?

10.04   What is the probability (p) of getting a head when you toss a symetrical coin?

10.05   How would certain events that may be described as "impossible" and "inevitable" be expressed using the notation of probability theory?

10.06   If it rains six days out of seven in a certain city in the northern hemisphere during the winter season, what is the probability that it will not rain on Christmas Day?

10.07   If gasoline consumption at 70 miles an hour is double the consumption at 35 miles per hour, is the relationship between speed and gasoline consumption linear?

10.08   Does this expression represent a linear programming problem:
$$ax^2 + bx + c = 0 \quad \ldots?$$

10.09   In a transportation problem, is there a feasible solution if
(a) supply exceeds demand? (b) demand exceeds supply?

10.10   What does the term "objective function" mean?

10.11   Solve the following generalized linear programming problem:

| Maximize | $x + y = z$ |
|---|---|
| Given that | $x + 2y = 8$ |
| Subject to the restraints: | $0 \leq x \leq 6$ |
| | $0 \leq y \leq 3$ |

That is, you are restricted in your solution to values of x which lie between (and include) 0 and 6, and values of y which lie between (and include) 0 and 3. (A graphical solution is acceptable).

10.12   A plastic cup manufacturer produces hot drink cups in two sizes, a small 7 oz. cup and a medium size 10 oz. cup.

The profit contribution is $2.50 per thousand on the small cups, and $3.00 per thousand on the medium cups.

Restraints on production and other facilities are as follows:

— the plant can produce a maximum of 350,000 small cups or 250,000 medium cups per day;

— the packaging equipment can handle 200,000 small cups or 300,000 medium cups per day;

— the Shipping Department can only cope with 150,000 small cups or 230,000 medium cups per day (more operations are involved in packing the tubes of small cups into cartons than for the medium cups).

What combination of small and medium cups should be produced daily to maximize profit contribution, assuming there are no limits on the quantity of each size that can be sold? (Again, the problem may be solved graphically.)

# APPENDIX A

## THE MATHEMATICAL CHARACTERISTICS
## OF DECLINING BALANCE DEPRECIATION

---

It is to be noted that the capital cost allowances under Canadian income tax regulations form a geometric series.

Thus, let $C$ = the original cost or capital cost of an asset.

$d$ = the applicable rate of depreciation or capital cost allowance.

The dollar amount of depreciation in each year, then, is as follows:

$$\text{Year } 1 = dC$$
$$2 = dC(1 - d)$$
$$3 = dC(1 - d)^2$$
$$\cdots\cdots\cdots\cdots$$
$$n = dC(1 - d)^{n-1}$$

. . . and the sum of the depreciation allowances over the life of the asset is a geometric progression, or:

$$S = dC[1 + (1 - d) + (1 - d)^2 + (1 - d)^3 + \ldots + (1 - d)^{n-1}]$$

It will be recalled that the nth term of a geomtric progression, or

$$t = ar^{n-1} \ldots \text{ and the sum of the series}$$

$$S = \frac{a(1 - r^n)}{1 - r}$$

where "a" is the first term and "r" is the common factor by which the 2nd and subsequent terms are multiplied to form the progression.

With a knowledge of these characteristics, the undepreciated capital cost of an asset, or the depreciation in any given year can be readily calculated.

Thus, the sum of the capital cost allowance up to and including year "n" (assuming the maximum is claimed in each year) is:

$$S = C[1 - (1 - d)^n] \qquad \text{(note 1)}$$

... The depreciation in any given year is:

$$t = dC(1 - d)^{n-1}$$

... And the undepreciated capital cost at the end of the nth year is:

$$C = C(1 - d)^n \qquad \text{(note 2)}$$

EXAMPLE:

Assume a machine (Class 8, 20%) having an original cost of $10,000 was purchased before March 30, 1966: what will be its undepreciated capital cost at the end of 1970, or after capital cost allowances have been claimed for 5 years?

*Solution:*

$$\begin{aligned} C_5 &= 10,000(1 - .20)^5 \\ &= 10,000(.80)^5 \\ &= 10,000(.32768) \\ &= \$3,276.80 \end{aligned}$$

Similarly, the answer to the question, "what would be the capital cost allowance in year 5?" is given by:

$$\begin{aligned} t_5 &= dC(1 - d)^4 \\ &= 2,000 \,(.80)^4 \\ &= 2,000 \,(.4096) \\ &= \$819.20 \end{aligned}$$

---

Note (1) $\quad S = \dfrac{dC[1 - (1 - d)^n]}{1 - (1 - d)} = C[1 - (1 - d)^n]$

(2) $\quad \begin{aligned} C &= C - S \\ &= C - C[1 - (1 - d)^n] \\ &= C - C + C\,(1 - d)^n \\ &= C(1 - d)^n \end{aligned}$

For large values of "n" it may be convenient to use logarithims to obtain the value of $r^n$ if a calculator or set of tables is not available.

Thus, it will be recalled that:

$$A^n = n\text{Log A}$$

$$\text{Hence } (.80)^5 = 5\text{Log}(.80)$$

$$= 5 \times \bar{1}.90309$$

$$= \bar{1}.51545$$

$$\text{Antilog } (\bar{1}.51545) = .32768$$

• • •

# TABLE OF POWERS: $(1 - d)^n$

| CLASS 10, 30% | | | CLASS 8, 20% | | | CLASS 6, 10% | | |
|---|---|---|---|---|---|---|---|---|
| | (n) | | | (n) | | | (n) | |
| (.70) | 2 | .49 | (.80) | 2 | .64 | (.90) | 2 | .81 |
| | 3 | .343 | | 3 | .512 | | 3 | .729 |
| | 4 | .2401 | | 4 | .4096 | | 4 | .6561 |
| | 5 | .16807 | | 5 | .32768 | | 5 | .59049 |
| | 6 | .117649 | | 6 | .262144 | | 6 | .531441 |
| | 7 | .082354 | | 7 | .209715 | | 7 | .478297 |
| | 8 | .057648 | | 8 | .167772 | | 8 | .430467 |
| | 9 | .040354 | | 9 | .134218 | | 9 | .387420 |
| | 10 | .028248 | | 10 | .107374 | | 10 | .348678 |
| | | | | | | | | |
| | 11 | .019774 | | 11 | .085899 | | 11 | .313810 |
| | 12 | .013842 | | 12 | .068719 | | 12 | .282429 |
| | 13 | .009689 | | 13 | .054975 | | 13 | .254186 |
| | 14 | .006782 | | 14 | .043980 | | 14 | .228767 |
| | 15 | .004747 | | 15 | .035184 | | 15 | .205890 |
| | 16 | .003323 | | 16 | .028147 | | 16 | .185301 |
| | 17 | .002326 | | 17 | .022518 | | 17 | .166771 |
| | 18 | .001628 | | 18 | .018014 | | 18 | .150094 |
| | 19 | .001140 | | 19 | .014411 | | 19 | .135085 |
| | 20 | .000798 | | 20 | .011529 | | 20 | .121577 |
| | | | | | | | | |
| | | | | | | | 21 | .109419 |
| | | | | | | | 22 | .098477 |
| | | | | | | | 23 | .088629 |
| | | | | | | | 24 | .079766 |
| | | | | | | | 25 | .071789 |
| | | | | | | | 26 | .064610 |
| | | | | | | | 27 | .058149 |
| | | | | | | | 28 | .052334 |
| | | | | | | | 29 | .047101 |
| | | | | | | | 30 | .042391 |
| | | | | | | | | |
| | | | | | | | 31 | .038152 |
| | | | | | | | 32 | .034337 |
| | | | | | | | 33 | .030903 |
| | | | | | | | 34 | .027815 |
| | | | | | | | 35 | .025032 |
| | | | | | | | 36 | .022529 |
| | | | | | | | 37 | .020276 |
| | | | | | | | 38 | .018248 |
| | | | | | | | 39 | .016423 |
| | | | | | | | 40 | .014781 |

# TABLE OF POWERS: $(1-d)^n$

### CLASS 3, 5%

| | (n) | | | (n) | |
|---|---|---|---|---|---|
| (.95) | 2 | .9025 | (.95) | 26 | .263520 |
| | 3 | .857375 | | 27 | .250344 |
| | 4 | .814506 | | 28 | .237827 |
| | 5 | .773781 | | 29 | .225936 |
| | 6 | .735092 | | 30 | .214639 |
| | 7 | .698337 | | | |
| | 8 | .663420 | | 31 | .203907 |
| | 9 | .630249 | | 32 | .193712 |
| | 10 | .598737 | | 33 | .184026 |
| | | | | 34 | .174825 |
| | 11 | .568800 | | 35 | .166084 |
| | 12 | .540360 | | 36 | .157780 |
| | 13 | .513342 | | 37 | .149891 |
| | 14 | .487675 | | 38 | .142396 |
| | 15 | .463291 | | 39 | .135276 |
| | 16 | .440126 | | 40 | .128512 |
| | 17 | .418120 | | | |
| | 18 | .397214 | | 41 | .122086 |
| | 19 | .377353 | | 42 | .115982 |
| | 20 | .358485 | | 43 | .110183 |
| | | | | 44 | .104674 |
| | 21 | .340561 | | 45 | .099440 |
| | 22 | .323533 | | 46 | .094468 |
| | 23 | .307356 | | 47 | .089745 |
| | 24 | .291988 | | 48 | .085258 |
| | 25 | .277389 | | 49 | .080995 |
| | | | | 50 | .076945 |

# APPENDIX B

## REPLIES TO SURVEY OF OPINION REGARDING THE MEANING OF THE TERMS "COST" AND "COST ACCOUNTING"

*1. A chartered accountant in public practice*

The *cost* of any given item or project represents the total expenditures, whether goods or services, of all components or elements of the given item or project. These expenditures must also include all fixed or variable overhead expenses that can properly be allocated as well as all direct expenditures required.

*Cost accounting* is the art of working with costs. This can include the accumulating recording, summarizing, presenting, comparing, tabulating or analysis of such costs. These functions can be performed on a regular systematic basis, or on an erratic basis, or once in a lifetime.

*2. A chartered accountant in industry*

The word *cost* has various meanings according to the situation. Generally, when viewed in terms of my personal affairs, it means the total purchase price or value for which a good or service is acquired. In such situations, I am aware that the cost to me is quite different than the actual cost to produce the good or service. This implies that there is an element of profit earned by the vendor and included in my cost. Normally in a business context or outside of my personal affairs, cost means the accumulated value of the good or service (arrived at) by combining labour, materials and overhead expenses. I do not consider cost as containing any element of profit in such instances. To me it then represents the sum value of direct and indirect components which affected its production.

*Cost accounting* represents the system whereby the elements of cost are classified, analyzed (and) compared to prior determined levels of realizable performance and deviations investigated. It indicates control and reporting on stewardship and might best be interpreted as "accounting for cost"—

i.e., where it came from, what it is made up of, etc. It represents a justification of the finished value of a produced good or service to which the vendor would hope to add a reasonable profit in order to merchandise it.

### 3. A professional engineer

*Cost* is the value of a unit of either goods or services in terms of the one-time dollar cost required to produce or purchase it.

*Cost accounting* is an organized system to allocate the total annual costs of operating a business (i.e., tangible and intangible costs) to the units of goods or services produced in order to determine the unit cost of production.

### 4. A records management consultant

*Cost* is a (total) figure representing the incurred charges for a product, a project or a programme. It implies merely a dollar and cents figure, nothing else.

*Cost accounting* is the term used to describe the cost analysis of any product, project or programme. Such analysis involves the estimation of all costs that may be incurred and would be broken down into labour, material and other operating expenses.

It is based on these figures that the mark-up is made and the selling price is determined.

*Cost accounting* also implies to me the concept of control so that after estimating the costs of labour, material and general operating expenses, a record of the actual costs is maintained and compared with the estimated costs. Only by such comparison can a realistic and accurate assessment be made of the cost accounting projections.

### 5. A marketing manager

*Cost* is the sum total of materials, labour, processing overhead, selling expense and all the other items that must enter into the production of a product or service.

*Cost accounting* is a technique by which the owners or managers of a business are enabled to determine the details of their operating, selling and incidental costs, and further, to project accurate determinations of the effects on the business of changes in volume, methods of distribution, scales of remuneration, and so forth.

I would think that, to the manager of a business (even a small one), an accurate and fast cost accounting system is as indispensable as an electrocardiograph (is) to a heart specialist. He can get along without one, but his patients' mortality rate is likely to be high.

### 6. A supermarket executive

In considering the word *cost* as applied to business transactions, I divide the term into two categories:

A. Expense incurred for the operation of the business concerned and always qualified in terms of the period of time such as "per day" or "per month," etc.

B. Expense applicable to the goods or service sold by the business concerned and expressed in terms of "per unit."

For category A, the general definition of cost is the net charge to income as a result of the operation involved—for example, the cost of window washing for the plant means to me the contractor's bill, if applicable, or if done by plant employees, (it) includes their time at wage cost plus fringe benefit overhead, plus the expense of materials used, etc.

For category B, the term *cost* is a compilation of the expenditures involved in producing an article or service for sale.

The term *cost accounting* to me means the intelligent application of accounting and statistical methods to the assembly of facts and figures required for costs.

In the case of category A costs, apart from making sure that all items are included in determining the proper application of overhead, interest, depreciation, etc., the cost accounting should achieve the most meaningful method of presentation to management of the costs of various operations by providing bases of measurement.

For category B, cost accounting involves, in addition to obvious expense compilation, the application of certain methods to preserve a consistent level of costs for the required period of time. For example, if selling prices are adjusted to a monthly schedule, costs should be so ordered as to eliminate fluctuations within the month due to such factors as overtime or a short number of working days, production interruptions, etc.

To sum up, the important factor of cost accounting, in my view, is the application of judgment to the arithmetical compilation so that distortions are eliminated.

# INDEX